The Rapture Question
Answered

The Rapture Question
Answered

Plain and Simple

Robert D. Van Kampen

Fleming H. Revell
A Division of Baker Book House
Grand Rapids, Michigan 49516

© 1997 by Robert Van Kampen

Published by Fleming H. Revell
a division of Baker Book House Company
P.O. Box 6287, Grand Rapids, MI 49516-6287

Third printing, April 1998

Printed in the United States of America

Library of Congress Cataloging-in-Publication Data

Van Kampen, Robert.
    The rapture question answered : plain and simple / Robert D.
Van Kampen.
      p. cm.
    Includes bibliographical references and indexes.
    ISBN 0-8007-1738-4 (cloth)
          0-8007-5631-2 (paper)
    1. Rapture (Christian eschatology) 2. Second Advent. I. Title.
BT887.V35 1997
236'.9—dc21   97-1677

All Bible quotations, unless otherwise indicated, are taken from the *New Ameri-
can Standard Bible*, copyright © 1977 by The Lockman Foundation.

For information about all releases from Baker Book House, visit our web site:
http://www.bakerbooks.com/

With great love and admiration,
I dedicate this book to my three daughters,
Kimberly Lynn Van Kampen, Kristen Joy Wisen,
and Karla Marlee Van Kampen-Pierre.
The joy of this father's heart
are his three precious gifts from God,
my three girls!

Contents

Acknowledgments

Three people in particular were of immense help to me in this project: Scott Carroll, without whose input on the Greek this book could never stand up to the scholarly scrutiny it is sure to be given; Charles Cooper, whose theological insight removed the secondary targets one might use to discredit the position argued in this book; and my wife, Judy, who must have read different stages of the manuscript at least ten times, encouraging me to argue the prewrath position clearly and logically.

Preface

In 1992, I wrote a theological book, *The Sign*, which attempted to harmonize all of the Old and New Testament prophetic passages concerning the end times. As such, *The Sign* is a very broad work dealing with many different aspects of the last days: Israel, the world in general, the church in general, the Day of the Lord, Antichrist and his ten-nation federation, and the true bond-servants of Christ who will be raptured at Christ's second coming. To date, the response to *The Sign:* approximately one hundred thousand copies of the book have been printed and distributed; it has been translated into Spanish and Russian; and a new ministry, The Sign Ministries, has been established to answer the tens of thousands of letters and phone calls we have received from readers.

The request most often made of us has been for a book dealing solely with the Rapture issue. Although this subject is certainly a part of *The Sign*, it is not specifically dealt with in a systematic manner intended to both explain and defend the position taken. To this end, therefore, *The Rapture Question Answered, Plain and Simple* was written.

If, indeed, the great hope of every believer is the second coming of Christ, something this important should be *clearly* taught in Scripture, especially in the New Testament. And, more important, this is something that every true child of God should know and understand! What the great hope of the church universal shouldn't be is a topic cloaked in confusion or a subject of heated debate that splits congregations and churches apart. Paul explains to Titus that those who are saved, should be "looking for the blessed hope and the appearing of the glory of our great God and Savior, Christ Jesus" (Titus 2:13; cf. 2 Pet. 3:12; 1 Thess. 5:4–6). That would be difficult to do if the Word of God didn't tell us specifically what to look for, or if His instructions concerning His second coming were so confusing that any attempt to understand "when" would be met with such heated debate that the true child of God would prefer to be ignorant on the issue rather than face the consequences.

The truth of the matter is, Scripture could not be clearer on this issue, not only as to the fact of Christ's coming and the judgment that will occur when He comes, but also the timing of His coming as it relates to other end time events.

Every attempt has been made to make this book both readable and interesting, in laypersons' terms, without sacrificing the importance of scholarship. Should you have any questions, I encourage you to call The Sign Ministries hot line (1-800-627-5134) or write to us at P.O. Box 113, West Olive, Michigan, 49460.

1

The Beginnings

Have you ever told someone a funny story you've just heard, only to find out he or she has already heard it several times in the past several months? Well, in the past ten years I have probably heard the same prophecy joke at least a hundred times, and in each instance, the teller has assumed I have never heard it before. It usually goes something like this. . . .

A person discovers that I have written a book on prophecy, and almost immediately he says, "You know, Bob, there are premillennialists, amillennialists, and postmillennialists. But I'm a panmillennialist myself." Not wishing to spoil his punch line, after just the right pause I ask, "So, what's a panmillennialist?" To which he responds with a grin, "It doesn't matter what I believe; it will all pan out in the end!"

There is, of course, a certain truth to that statement. But not only does it make light of a serious teaching of Scripture; it also, like most partial truths, creates an impression that is both false and misleading, adding to the indifference and confusion that many Christians already have about the end times—in particular, about the return of Christ for His saints. In light of this prevalent confusion, it is no wonder that average Christians often throw up their hands, not knowing what to believe. They conclude, perhaps even subconsciously, that things will indeed just "pan out" in the end, because regardless of what they believe, there is nothing they can do about it anyway.

Yet God's own Word tells us that He "is not a God of confusion" (1 Cor. 14:33). And because He does not want His people to be confused, His Word thoroughly reveals every truth we need in order to live our lives in certainty as well as in obedience. So why, we wonder, is there still so much confusion—even among those who sincerely hold to the inerrancy, authority, and sufficiency of Scripture—concerning an event as critical as the second coming of Christ?

The answer is incredibly simple. Since there can be *no confusion* in God's Word concerning the return of Christ (1 Cor. 14:33), the confusion obviously must come from our own incomplete and incorrect understanding of His Word.

As you will see in the following pages, the Bible is very specific concerning Christ's return for His own, including *when His return will occur in relation to other end time events*! It is our own faulty interpretation of Scripture, or, equally wrong, our unwillingness to accept what the Scriptures clearly teach, that causes all the confusion.

Sad to say, many students and teachers of prophecy seem willing to adopt almost any method of interpretation that sidesteps the obvious teaching of Scripture on this all-important matter. That is tragic, because "the appearing of the glory of our great God and Savior, Christ Jesus" is the great hope of the church (Titus 2:13). Scripture is abundantly clear concerning the return of Christ, and those who ignore its obvious teaching do great disservice to the body of Christ. But too often, the average Christian, simply and uncritically, believes what others write or preach, trusting the words of man instead of what is written in the Word of God. Yet the Bible is a book of absolutes, and whatever we hear and read must be measured by what God's Word says.

No sincere believer *wants* to be taken in by unbiblical prophetic ideas or other false teaching, and it is for such sincere and open-minded believers that this book was written. Except for one instance in the final chapter, I do not appeal to other writers who think as I do about this all-important Rapture issue. That can be the blind leading the blind. Rather, I have attempted to build my case entirely on Scripture, and I think you will be amazed at how clear and precise it really is concerning the return of Christ for His own.

Before we begin our study together, however, it may be helpful for you to know something about me, since certain aspects of my life will probably give you better insight into where I am coming from and how I came to the positions I have taken in this book. Let me explain.

My father was, among other things, a Christian publisher almost a half century ago. Through him and his work, I came in contact with many men who already were or who soon would become household names in conservative Christian circles. As I grew up, these men were often in our home, and I came to know most of them personally. Not only was I brought up to think biblically, but, through my father, I was given direct access to dynamic Christian leaders and to the organizations with which they were affiliated.

When I graduated from college, my interests were in commerce rather than full-time ministry. I firmly believe that God endows each of His children with special aptitudes that can be used equally well in commerce or ministry, because the same ability can be used in many different ways. In the business world, we use our aptitudes largely for our own edification and for the well-being of ourselves and our families. In ministry, we use our aptitudes (which may correspond to our spiritual gifts) for the edification and well-being of others, especially within the church. In both realms, however, we are responsible before the Lord as to how we use what He has given us.

My aptitudes are logical and analytical in nature. Over the years since college, I have started or have been a part of building several companies in the investment banking industry, specifically in money management for others where a logical, analytical mind was a necessity. Wishful thinking didn't bring in the necessary returns the investors demanded, nor did it pay the salaries of the employees. The scorecard was easy to keep. If you did your job right, you grew; if you didn't, you went out of business. Looking back, it appears to me that God used my natural aptitudes to prosper my business career in a way I could never have done on my own.

When I was in my twenties and just beginning to learn the business, I was tagged with the nickname "The Charger" by my co-workers. If I needed something, I went after it. If I wanted to know something, my charger personality and my analytical mind drove me until I got the answers.

As the years passed and my business interests grew, so did my visibility and outspoken commitment to the Word of God. As a result, I soon had many of the same contacts in the fields of ministry that my father had had. I knew the presidents of Christian organizations and colleges, many on a first-name basis. If I needed sound biblical or theological assistance on a certain issue, I could go directly to them or to professors on their faculties who could readily give me the help I needed. As would be expected, such access became a great asset in my work on eschatology—the study of the end times.

But there was a time, early in my adult life, when I didn't have the same confidence in God's Word that I have today. It was back in my college days, when my views and ideals were being challenged, molded, and shaped, and my quest for biblical truth was beginning. During those years, I attended a fine Christian college. Academically, the education was superb. But many professors in the science department taught that the creation account given in the first two chapters of Genesis could not be accepted as literal. In addition, because of the geological implications, they also taught that the Noahic Flood had to be local, not universal as the Bible stated. According to their view, while the biblical accounts of the creation and the Flood contained spiritual truth, neither of them was to be fully understood as a literal event because to do so would contradict scientific evidence. God did not create the earth and everything in it, including man, in a literal, six-day period of time; rather, God created through the process of evolution. They called their position *theistic evolution* because the position attempted to be biblical—which is why it is called *theistic*—while at the same time accommodating the evolutionary beliefs of the scientific community. These professors were brilliant men, and I was young and still impressionable. Without questioning, I accepted their position "hook, line, and sinker" because it seemed to be a logical solution to the dilemma I had been trying to come to terms with, bringing what I thought to be harmony to what the Bible said and what these men taught as scientific fact.

I married right after college, and although my wife and I moved around the country quite a bit during our first years of married life, we always sought out a good church to attend. And it was then that, for the first time in my life, I began to question certain old themes I was hearing from the pulpit. After all, I reasoned, if the biblical account of creation is not to be taken literally, and if the Noahic Flood was local, not universal as the text seemed to indicate, then other teachings of Scripture that I had always understood and accepted at face value needed to be challenged rather than blindly accepted.

Thus, I began the most important battle of my spiritual life. Were the concepts of heaven and hell to be understood literally, or, like creation, could they be spiritualized or allegorized away? Was Christ really God come to earth in the flesh, or was He simply a great man, a great teacher? Or was He truly the son of God but not God Himself? There came a time when I even wondered if the resurrection of Christ could really have occurred as recorded in Scripture since I knew that resurrection from the dead, like a literal six-day creation, was also a scientific impossibility.

But in spite of the confusion my science teachers had created in my mind, in my heart I knew that Christ was, indeed, fully God. I knew that heaven was real and that an awful, terrible hell awaited those who never received Christ as their Savior and Lord. What's more, I knew that Christ did rise from the dead after spending three days and three nights in the grave. Everything I believed by faith, in the depths of my soul, hinged upon trusting in those biblical truths, exactly as they were recorded by the writers of Scripture! Thus, I was beginning to realize that the very heart of my personal faith rested on the firm confidence that Scripture means exactly what it says.

It was during these days of confusion, six or seven years after I was married, that a college friend told me a story I have never forgotten. Because this was back in the sixties, you may already have heard it. But it had a great impact on my thinking then—and it still does today. Every Bible class I have taught over the years has heard it at some time or another. Probably several times! This is the story he told:

There was a certain farmer who raised watermelons. Each year the neighborhood kids would sneak into the farmer's field and steal his ripe melons. Finally, one year, determined to put a stop to this practice, the farmer waited until the watermelons were ripe and then put a small sign in the center of the patch: "Steal watermelons at your own risk. Beware! One is poisoned!" Several days later he went out to check his crop, and sure enough, not one watermelon had been stolen. But there was a second little sign in the center of the patch, right next to the first: "Now there are two!"

The warning the farmer thought would discourage the theft of a few watermelons had resulted in the loss of the entire patch! Because he had no way of knowing which other melon might be poisoned, the entire patch had become suspect.

That little story hit me right between the eyes. It illustrated the very dilemma in which I found myself. Taken literally, the Bible plainly teaches that God created the earth and everything on and above it in six, literal, twenty-four-hour days. And yet I had been taught that evolution was scientific fact and that the only position that could harmonize Scripture with science was the theistic evolution position, a position that could not accept the creation account recorded in Genesis as literal. How then, I wondered, can the Bible be trustworthy in matters of faith if it is so far off the mark in matters of science? How do we know which passages of Scripture are to be understood allegorically or spiritually, and which passages should be understood literally? And who decides which ones are interpreted which way, especially if the passage itself gives the reader no clear indication that it should be understood in any manner other than at face value? How was I to resolve the dilemma between science and faith?

By now the battle for my logical, analytical mind was well underway, for I was beginning to realize that when you spiritualize or allegorize even a few passages of Scripture, you cast doubt on the meaning of all the rest of the passages that should be understood at face value. Like the watermelon patch, the whole Bible becomes suspect. *If you can't trust all of it at face value, you can't trust any of it, because you have no means of determining what can be understood at face value and what needs to be understood spiritually or allegorically.*

At about this same time, another good friend told me about a book on creationism written by a man of impeccable academic and scientific credentials. In this book, the author carefully showed how the Bible, when taken for exactly what it says, is as trustworthy scientifically as it is theologically.

As I studied this man's scientific arguments for accepting the written Word at face value, I came to realize that evolution, like creationism, is no more than a theory when it comes to origins. It is anything but fact! For any theory to be recognized as scientific fact, it must be tested and demonstrated as reliable through consistent, repeatable, and observable results. Because both the creation and evolution positions acknowledge that man came on the scene at the end of a chain of events associated with origins, both sides agree that there were no eyewitnesses to our beginnings. As neither the claims of creationism nor evolutionism have ever been verified by replication, *both positions must remain theories*, by definition, until replication of either of these theories can be achieved and witnessed on a repeatable basis. Until that can be accomplished, all we can do is compare our theories—evolution and creation—against the scientific facts we do have. This is when the creationist gives the evolutionist real nightmares! The foundational laws of science—the First and Second Laws of Thermodynamics—support a completed creation rather than an ongoing evolutionary process, and a created world corrupted by the Fall that is slowly running down rather than a world that is constantly improving because of the evolution of all things to a higher level. In addition, the layer upon layer of similar stratification seen across the world, obviously deposited by water, is far better explained by a worldwide flood as described in the book of Genesis than by the various imaginative accounts used by the evolutionist to explain away the obvious!

In my opinion, any sensible and honest mind has to recognize that every design must have a designer. Without a designer, we have chaos. And there is no design more complex, beautiful, and self-evident than that of our world, including our own design as human beings. On that evidence of creation alone, God holds all humankind "without excuse" as to their knowledge of His existence and power (Rom. 1:20). Thus, I became convinced that God meant exactly what He said in the creation account, the Flood account, and every other account that He took the time to include in His Word!

Resolving my creation dilemma became the catalyst for my aggressive defense of the reliability of the Bible as God's inerrant Word when taken and understood at face value. However, I quickly learned that most Christians struggle with the simplicity of that position. *The debate among most conservative, evangelical Christians is not over the inerrancy or the authority of Scripture, but over how the Bible is to be interpreted—as the creation–evolution debate attests.*

Yet Paul instructed the church at Corinth that "we write nothing else to you than what you read and understand, and I hope you will understand until the end" (2 Cor. 1:13). In other words, if they could read it, they could understand it. All a believer needs is eyes to read or ears to hear with. That is the fundamental hermeneutic every believer should employ, because that is God's divinely revealed method for studying and understanding His divinely revealed truth.

A Face-Value Hermeneutic

Because I will use the term *hermeneutic* often throughout this book, a word of explanation is necessary. One's hermeneutic basically refers to how one understands something that is written or spoken. *The normal method we use every day is what I refer to as the "face-value hermeneutic": we understand what we read or hear by taking what is said to us at face value—or, by taking it literally, if you prefer that word—in its most natural, normal, customary sense.*

As I look back on my years of wrestling with the Word of God, I have come to realize that the only hermeneutic that makes the Bible alive and meaningful is the hermeneutic that takes Scripture exactly for what it says. That doesn't mean that we are to ignore the many obvious figures of speech and expressions that are found in Scripture, but that does eliminate spiritualization (substituting the literal sense for a deeper, spiritual meaning), allegorization (abandoning the literal sense for what the reader considers to be a more meaningful understanding), culturalization (limiting unnecessarily the literal sense to the culture of the day in which it was written), and any other scheme that distorts what the text says when understood in its most normal, natural, customary sense.

Those who take it upon themselves to change the obvious meaning to something less obvious have, in my opinion, a kind of God-complex. Like God, *they* have the right to make the text mean whatever *they* would like it to mean instead of what the Author intended it to mean. It is my firm belief that the true meaning of any text can only be understood when that text is taken at face value, in context, harmonized with all the other passages of Scripture speaking to the same issue. When that meaning is found, that meaning stands in judgment of us. Never do we dare stand in judgment of it! (I read that last comment years ago in a book by Dr. A. W. Tozer, and it has been a part of my theological thinking ever since.)

Let me explain the face-value hermeneutic another way: *if the plain sense makes sense, you have the right sense.* If this simple little rule were used by those who love and study God's Word, much of the confusion concerning end time events would not exist. But, sad to say, teachers too often approach prophecy using the method of interpretation that best suits their own biases or circumstances rather than accepting the clear intent of the biblical writer.

Scripture Never Contradicts Scripture

Our responsibility as students of the Word is to make every attempt to understand what is written in its most natural, normal, customary sense, being careful to first look at all other passages that deal with whatever particular issue we are studying. *Remember—and this is critical—we have not found truth*

until we find the single common denominator that makes all of
the passages fit together. Psalm 119:160 teaches us that "the
sum of Thy word is truth." In other words, you don't have truth
until you have processed all of the passages dealing with a particular subject and found the single solution that accommo-
dates them all without contradiction!

I often explain it this way. Assume you have six passages
dealing with a particular topic. Using the face-value hermeneutic, passages 1, 3, and 5 say one thing, while passages 2, 4, and
6 appear, on the surface, to be saying something quite different.
Those who prefer what 1, 3, and 5 have to say conclude that the
common denominator that pulls these three passages together is
15, and on 15 they will stand and give their life, if necessary,
sweeping passages 2, 4, and 6 under the rug, so to speak. On the
other hand, those who prefer what passages 2, 4, and 6 have to
say come to the common denominator of 12, and they, like their
counterparts, are willing to die for their position, irrespective of
what the three other passages might have to say on the issue at
hand.

Which answer is right? 12 or 15? Actually, neither is right!
If you want truth, you cannot ignore any of the passages that
deal with the same issue, no matter how contradictory they
may seem. However, if you refuse to be sidetracked by the
contradiction and keep looking for the resolution, you will
eventually find that all the passages fit perfectly into one common denominator: 60. Now you have correlation without contradiction. Now you have truth!

Until the common denominator is found, you don't have anything except confusion. Plain and simple. Until then, you must
simply admit that you don't know. That's the best answer to
give when you're not sure! Then you keep looking for that single solution that makes all the passages come together perfectly, without contradiction.

Figures of Speech

It must be remembered, of course, that the Bible uses *figures of speech*. A figure of speech is "any deviation either in thought or expression, from the ordinary and simple method of speaking . . . a form of speech artfully varied from common usage."[1] *A figure of speech will normally employ a comparison, a substitution, or an amplification* as a means of "artfully varying" from what we think of as common use, to better clarify the passage. *If the plain sense doesn't make sense, you're probably dealing with some sort of a figure of speech, which the context or the rest of Scripture will define for you!* It is important for us to understand figures of speech because they are used often in prophetic texts. Let me illustrate each of these types. Once understood, they normally can be recognized quite easily.

Comparison

There are three common examples of figures of speech that are comparative in nature. The only hard part to understand about these three figures are the names someone—not me—has tacked onto them: similes, metaphors, and idioms. The toughest part is the names. *The important thing is to know a figure of speech when you see one, not the technical term for it.*

Similes are the easiest to recognize. The comparison is direct. Connecting words such as *like* or *as* compare two things or thoughts for the purpose of greater clarification. In Revelation 1:14, for example, Christ is described as one whose "head and His hair were white like white wool, *like* snow; and His eyes were *like* a flame of fire" (emphasis added). This doesn't mean His hair was actually snow, but that it looked like snow. In the same way, His eyes were not fire, literally, but were like a flame of fire.

1. Instit. Orat. IX, I. 11, cited by Edward P. J. Corbett, *Classical Rhetoric for the Modern Student* (New York: Oxford Press, 1971), 640.

Metaphors, a second common example of a comparative figure of speech, employ an implied comparison rather than a direct comparison like similes do. There are no connecting words. Revelation 12:4 states, "And the dragon stood before the woman who was ready to give birth." Taken at face value, the plain sense doesn't really make sense. An actual dragon doesn't seem to be in keeping with the rest of the passage so the reader must look at the surrounding context for clarification. A few verses later we are told that "the great dragon was thrown down, the serpent of old who is called the devil and Satan" (v. 9), thus explaining the figure of speech used a few verses earlier. This is the vivid picture the author wants his reader to have in his mind when thinking of Satan and so to accomplish this, he uses a metaphor which, in no way, detracts from the face-value understanding of this passage.

Another thing to remember is that different metaphors—such as a dragon or a serpent—are sometimes used in Scripture to describe the same person or thing, each one giving the reader a different but more thorough understanding of the important characteristics of the subject matter at hand. Jesus Christ is depicted in various places as the Son of God, the Lamb, the Lion, the Good Shepherd, and the King of kings. These metaphors, although quite varied, give the reader a more complete picture of Christ and the role He plays throughout history.

To further illustrate this use of the metaphor with a subject matter we will be looking at in some detail in the following chapters, Scripture depicts the man we commonly refer to as Antichrist using a number of different metaphors. Actually, you may be surprised to know that the term *Antichrist* is used only once in the first epistle of John to describe this exceedingly powerful and evil man who will stand against Christ in the end times. The term is never used in books that are heavily prophetic, such as the book of Revelation. Instead, in this final book of the Bible the term most often used of Antichrist is *beast.*

In addition, titles such as the man of lawlessness, the son of destruction, the one who makes desolate, and prince are also used for Antichrist, each giving us a better understanding of the nature and character of this end time figure who is so intent on destroying the elect of God!

In a similar way, but at the opposite end of the spiritual spectrum, this book will often differentiate between genuine Christians and the church in general. Although the word *Christian* is used only three times in the entire New Testament, the New Testament writers often refer to genuine Christians as the elect, the body of Christ, the children of God, the chosen, saints, bond-servants, brethren, those who have eyes to see and ears to hear, and overcomers. Interestingly, the word *church* (in its local sense) is most often used to describe a group of professing Christians, many of whom may or may not be the genuine children of God (see Rev. 3:1–7). In chapter 7, when we look more closely at the book of Revelation, this distinction in terminology becomes critical.

The point I am trying to make is this: different writers may use different words to describe the same person or thing. These are figures of speech and do not detract from the natural, normal, customary sense—that is, the face-value sense—of the passage in which these figures of speech are being used. Instead, *when the plain sense doesn't make sense, Scripture must be compared with Scripture, letting Scripture determine the meaning of the comparative language being used by the author.* Once you learn how certain writers use certain metaphors, you will find that there is normally a consistent use of those metaphors throughout their writings. Remember: *the Bible is always the best dictionary for explaining itself.*

Idioms are the last example of comparative figures of speech. Idioms are basically what we think of today as expressions, not unlike those words and phrases we use in normal, everyday conversation. When Paul refers to his "thorn in the flesh" (2 Cor. 12:7), he doesn't mean that a thorn was literally embedded in his flesh, but rather, as the context goes on to say, he is referring to "a messenger of Satan [given] to buffet me—to keep me from exalting myself." When Christ said to Saul, "It is hard for thee to kick against the pricks" (Acts 26:14, KJV), the plain sense doesn't seem to make sense. Why? Because Christ was using an idiom—an expression—to question Saul's past opposition to Christ. The time had come for Saul to face up to reality!

Like the above examples, some expressions will be explained *in* the context, others *by* the context, but in each case, expressions are to be understood as such. We all use expressions in our everyday conversations without distorting the face-value meaning of what we are trying to convey to others. So do the writers of Scripture. As you have perhaps already noted, I am prone to use expressions often, but not at the detriment of the face-value understanding of what I am trying to communicate.

Substitution

The second category of figures of speech is substitutionary in nature. The most common example of this figure is called a *metonymy*. I realize that the handle—metonymy—is tough and to be perfectly candid with you, spotting one may be tougher yet. In this case, I think one example may be far better than a thousand words of explanation:

In Psalm 23:5, David states, "You prepare a *table* before me." By "table" he means a feast on a table. David substituted "table" for "feast." Why, I don't know. But it is clear that David meant to say more than God put plates, knives, forks, and spoons on a table. Rather, God prepared a feast for David in front of his enemies, making the point that God superabundantly blessed David even in the very presence of his enemies. Enough said about metonymies!

Amplification

The third category of figures of speech uses amplification in order to make the underlying meaning of the text more clear. This figure of speech, like the comparative figure of speech, is easy to spot. In this case, an idea or thing is stated and then that idea or thing is clarified—or amplified—by the addition of more information. This is called *parallelism.*

Parallelism is most often employed in poetical writings like Psalms and Proverbs. As the word *parallel* would seem to indicate, parallelism consists normally of two separate thoughts, side by side, used in tandem with one another to bring greater meaning to the text. Parallelism is structured around several basic patterns. Notice for an example, Psalm 2:4:

> He that sits in the heavens will laugh,
> Yahweh will hold them in derision.

In this example, these two lines mean exactly the same thing. That is one very common pattern used in parallelism. But opposite or contrasting thoughts can also be used. We find this contrasting usage in Psalm 1:6. Here, the Psalmist says:

> For Yahweh knows the way of the righteous
> but the way of the wicked will perish.

In this example, these two lines mean the exact opposite. Therefore, as we can see, parallelism is used to amplify the meaning of the first line by restating the same truth in the second line, only differently; or to amplify the meaning of the first line by offering a contrast, an opposite idea or truth, in the second line.

In addition to parallel thoughts, in the original languages the parallel sentences will also tend to be approximately the same length, whether measured in terms of words or syllables. Much of this meter, however, is lost in the translation from the Hebrew or Greek to the English.

In Context

Equally important as understanding Scripture in its most natural, normal, customary sense is understanding Scripture in the overall context of what the writer is saying. Only when you know the context will you know how the writer intended the passage to be understood. A common danger is what is commonly called prooftexting: building an interpretation on the superficial application of a biblical text taken out of context.

For example, Luke quotes Jesus as saying, "Soul, you have many goods laid up for many years to come; take your ease, eat, drink and be merry" (12:19). An extreme example of taking a text out of context would be to use that statement to justify a selfish, hedonistic lifestyle. But in its proper context, Christ goes on to say in the following verse, "But God said to him, 'You fool! This very night your soul is required of you.'" The text has a completely different meaning when its context is taken into consideration.

Let Scripture Define Scripture

The final point that I would make reference to is a point we have already referred to earlier, numerous times. In the following pages of this book, this principle will be used, again and again. *Let Scripture define Scripture; let the Bible be your dictionary.* This is true whenever you study God's Word. It is especially true when you study end times. The book of Revelation in particular is loaded with figures of speech, especially comparative language that should never be allegorized but instead realized by searching the Scriptures for the explanation of what is meant by the passage in question. When you let Scriptures interpret Scriptures, you build your case on what the Word of God says. When you let man interpret Scripture, you build your case on what that particular man thinks and anything goes, especially truth!

Over the years I have often been challenged because of the strong positions I take on several very controversial matters. When I take these positions, I have done my homework in advance, being sure that I have looked at all the passages dealing with the particular issue at hand, using the hermeneutic described in the preceding pages. It is always a particular delight to me when I can point to chapter and verse, then tell my accuser that the issue is not with me, but with what the Scriptures clearly say. Usually that puts an end to the conversation.

Summing It Up

In my opinion there is only one legitimate hermeneutic we can use if we seek to know the truth of God's Word. *The text must be understood at face value, in its most natural, normal, customary sense, making allowances for obvious figures of speech, its context, and all the other passages of Scripture dealing with the same issue. When in doubt, let Scripture interpret Scripture! Once the common denominator is found that harmonizes all the passages, without contradiction, then we have truth, but not before. And once we have truth, that truth stands in judgment of us; never do we dare stand in judgment of it!*

In 2 Corinthians 1:13, Paul was writing to the common people of Corinth, many of whom were uneducated. In essence, the apostle was telling these believers that if they had eyes to read God's Word or ears to hear it, they could understand it. God's Word was written plainly and simply in order that plain and simple people like you and me, without theological degrees, can understand it.

If we follow this simple, face-value hermeneutic, we will never have reason to be ashamed or embarrassed—on any issue! Scripture will become practical and useful, speaking to every facet of our lives, from spiritual issues to family, to interpersonal relationships, to business, to science, to history, to psychology, to health, to law, and, more to the point of this book, to the timing of the Rapture—Christ's wondrous return to take His own to be with Him—the great hope of the church. But to do this, each one of us is required to "be diligent to present [himself or herself] approved to God as a workman who does not need to be ashamed, *handling accurately the word of truth*" (2 Tim. 2:15, emphasis added).

It was because they had such unreserved reverence for and trust in God's Word that the Bereans were commended as being "more noble-minded than those in Thessalonica, for they received the word with great eagerness, examining the Scriptures daily, to see whether these things were so" (Acts 17:11).

As you work through this study with me, I ask only that you be like the Bereans. Examine the Scriptures to see if these things are so.

The Issues

Over the years I found that almost every critical biblical issue could be resolved by using the hermeneutic described in the previous chapter. But the timing of the Rapture, Christ's return for His own, eluded me. Not surprising, I suppose, since it has always been an unsettled, controversial issue, even among scholars who hold to the face-value hermeneutic. I had endless conversations on the subject with my friends who were professors of Bible at Moody Bible Institute. Many of them lived in the western suburbs of Chicago and would catch the train down to Chicago's Loop every day, as I did. So I always kept an eye out for them. I had lots of questions, and I figured they had the answers, or at least could point me in the right direction. If they saw me first, though, they soon began ducking behind their newspapers or the people sitting in front of them! They knew what I wanted, and what I wanted wasn't what they wanted. I wanted answers; they wanted to make use of this time to grade papers, prepare class work, or just relax before the rat race at school began.

When we did connect, my "charger" personality took over. I wanted to know what Scripture taught

concerning anything and everything, and, because of the un-
resolved issues I had in my own mind, I had lots of questions
concerning eschatology—the study of end time events. When
they gave me their answer, invariably, my next question was
almost automatic: "Is that your opinion, or is that what the
Bible teaches?" When they told me that their position was
what Scripture taught, my counter was equally predictable:
"Show me where!" You might say that much of my thinking on
biblical issues was train trained!

I had known one of these professors since our college
days together. Often we continued our train conversations
in one another's homes, sitting on the living room floor, our
Bibles and concordances spread out in front of us, wrestling
with the texts that concerned the events that will occur in
the last days, in particular, the timing of Christ's return for
His saints.

By this time I had become thoroughly convinced that God
means precisely what He says, so the amillennial and the post-
millennial positions concerning the return of Christ were never
ones I seriously considered. Both of those positions are driven
largely by an allegorical hermeneutic that was unacceptable to
me, because their conclusions were always different than what
the text appeared to be saying if taken at face value. In both instances the clear references in Scripture to a literal thousand-
year rule of Christ over a literal kingdom upon earth were completely discarded in favor of their own private interpretation of
what the text really meant to say. Because the allegorical
method of interpretation depends upon what the reader thinks
rather than what the writer wrote, it was often difficult for those
holding to such an allegorical interpretation to even agree
among themselves on key issues. Once Scripture is subject to
man's interpretation—the thrust of the allegorical method—the
question then becomes, *Which interpretation of which man does
one use?* Because of my hermeneutic, there was but one meaning

to the text and that was the meaning intended by the writer of the text, not the reader, plain and simple.

Before Christ came to earth the first time, there were hundreds of Old Testament prophecies that foretold His coming. Well over fifty individual aspects of His life and death were foretold, including the place of His birth, His lineage, His ministry, His death, the method by which He would die, and His burial and resurrection, to name but a few. It is interesting to note that when Christ came, each one of these Old Testament prophecies was fulfilled at face value. That exact fulfillment is one of the strongest evidences that Jesus was, indeed, the Messiah promised in the Old Testament. And if the prophecies concerning Christ's first coming were fulfilled at face value, I reasoned, why would the prophecies concerning His second coming be fulfilled any differently?

In my opinion, any fulfillment of prophecy other than a face-value fulfillment is meaningless. If someone predicts that something is going to happen in a certain way, at a certain time, and then it doesn't happen that way, he obviously is no prophet and his predictions are worthless. It's as simple as that. Only when predictions are fulfilled exactly as stated do we gain confidence in the one making the predictions. And, in this writer's opinion, that is exactly how prophecy concerning the second coming of Christ should be understood.

Certain Things We Could Agree Upon

The most popular face-value position concerning Christ's second coming, taught in most conservative evangelical churches, Bible schools, and seminaries, is called *premillennialism*. This position teaches that there will be a literal thousand-year reign of Christ over a literal kingdom on earth that He will establish after the events associated with His second coming. Revelation 20 refers no less than six times to this thousand-year reign of Christ (in particular, see v. 4). As the name implies, premillennialism holds that Christ will return to earth *before* (pre-) His thousand-year (millennial) reign over earth. Because of my hermeneutic, I had to be premillennial, and on this issue my friends and I had no disagreement.

Those who hold to the premillennial return of Christ also agree that just prior to the thousand-year reign of Christ there will be a seven-year period of trouble on earth, beginning mildly and increasing in intensity as this period progresses. This period is referred to, in part, by Christ in His Olivet Discourse recorded in the book of Matthew (24:3–31), described in more detail in the final chapters of the prophetic book of Daniel (11:36–12:13), and fleshed out in great detail by John in the book of Revelation. This final, seven-year period of time is normally referred to by teachers of eschatology as the *tribulation period*.

As already noted, because of my literal hermeneutic I had to be premillennial, believing that Christ will return for His saints before He comes to reign over His kingdom on earth for a thousand years. For the same reason, I had to believe in the tribulation period, a preceding seven-year period of time that would be marked by worldwide tribulation of one sort or another. So far, my friends and I were in total agreement.

Agreement also came easily concerning a subdivision of that seven-year tribulation period. Again, as before, because of Christ's teaching in the Olivet Discourse (Matt. 24:15, 21–22), the teaching of Daniel (Dan. 9:27; 12:1, 6–12), and the teaching of the book of Revelation (in particular, chapter 13), I knew that the *last half* of this seven-year tribulation period would be dominated by a *very real, living man*—whom the apostle John refers to as *Antichrist* or *the beast*. The seven-year tribulation period will begin when this man who becomes Antichrist makes a seven-year treaty with Israel, who will, once again, be living in her own homeland when this treaty is signed (Dan. 9:27). Three-and-a-half years later, those who refuse to worship Antichrist or refuse to take his

RAPTURE POSITIONS

Daniel's Seventieth Week

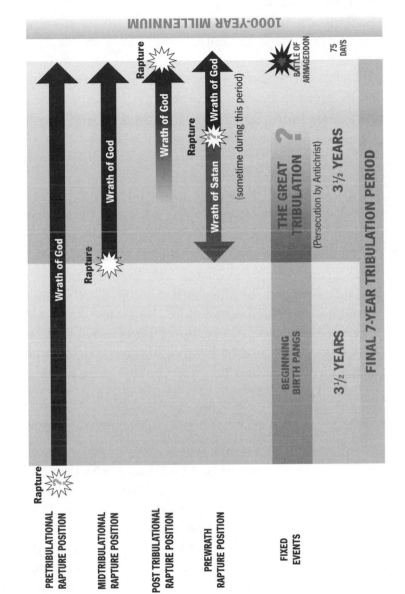

mark (666) will become the targets of his severe persecution, a persecution unlike any the elect of God has ever known. Antichrist's unprecedented persecution of the elect of God (Matt. 24:21) and the nation of Israel (Dan. 12:1), which initiates the final half of the seven-year tribulation period, is referred to as a time of *great tribulation,* the term Christ specifically gives to this time of intense persecution in His Olivet Discourse to His disciples (Matt. 24:21). And, once again, my friends and I were still in total agreement. We applied the same hermeneutic to the same passages and came to the same conclusions.

We could even agree on the general timing of the battle of Armageddon. This final great showdown—Christ and His heavenly armies against Antichrist and his earthly armies— will be the climax of God's wrath (Rev. 19:11–21; cf. 15:1), occurring on a single day just shortly before the onset of the Millennial Kingdom of Christ (Rev. 20). That's the nice thing about a face-value hermeneutic. When the text is clear, agreement comes easily . . . or does it? I was soon to find out that my friends believed in a face-value hermeneutic only as long as it agreed with what they had been taught, were teaching, or were expected to believe by others whose approval was more important than what the Scriptures appeared to teach. When the hermeneutic shifted away from a simple, face-value understanding of what the text was saying, explanations got longer and longer and emotions got hotter and hotter! Let me explain.

The overriding question every student of eschatology has to face and ultimately deal with is this: *Will the church have to face this intense time of persecution by Antichrist, or will she be removed before this time referred to as a "great tribulation" ever begins?* More often than not, it is upon this issue that the battle lines are drawn and the wars are fought! This is a burning question still being debated today in the halls of theological thinking across the land. Not surprisingly, then, this became *the* question behind the heated debates my friends and I had concerning the timing of Christ's return.

Pre, Post, or What?

By far the most popular Rapture[1] position taught by those who would say that they agree with a face-value hermeneutic is called the pretribulation Rapture position. Because adherents to this position believe that Christ will come for His church *before* the seven-year tribulation period begins, they obviously believe that the church will not experience the persecution by Antichrist during that terrible time that Christ specifically refers to in the Olivet Discourse and that John describes in the book of Revelation. Thus the name *pre* (before) *tribulation* (the tribulation period). Those holding this position teach that the rapture of the saints can occur at any moment— what they refer to as *imminency*—but it must occur *before* the tribulation period commences. This was the position of my friends who taught at Moody Bible Institute.

A far smaller group of evangelical teachers of prophecy argue that the rapture of the saints will not occur until the very end of the tribulation period, meaning that the church will undergo persecution at the hands of Antichrist. That position is therefore most commonly called the *post* (after) *tribulation* Rapture position. Several of my friends who taught at Trinity Seminary in Deerfield, Illinois, held to this position.

An even smaller group of evangelical theologians hold to a midtribulation Rapture position. It shouldn't be hard to figure out when they think the Rapture will occur. In their view, the church will experience the less severe problems associated with the first half of the tribulation period but not the immensely worse persecution at the hands of Antichrist during

1. Although *rapture* is the term we use to describe this end time event, the term itself never appears in Scripture. It is from the Latin word *raptus*, meaning "a dragging or taking away, a violent rending."

the second half. Because the interpretive assumptions of the pretribulationists are basically the same as those of the midtribulationists—both positions keeping the church out of Antichrist's severe persecution—I have, for the sake of simplicity, lumped the two positions together and in the following pages refer to them as the pretribulation Rapture position.

Since I had been taught that the pretribulation and posttribulation positions were the only two real options concerning when the Rapture could occur if indeed Scripture was to be taken and understood at face value, I quickly became thoroughly confused and frustrated. Unlike the clear teachings of Scripture concerning the end time issues we could agree upon—the millennium, the seven-year tribulation period, the great tribulation persecution of Antichrist, and Armageddon—I could not find either the pretribulation or posttribulation timing of the Rapture taught anywhere in Scripture although *both sides* had elements of truth that Scripture did support. My problem wasn't with those areas of their position that had strong, biblical support, but rather I had a problem with those parts that contradicted other passages of Scripture, speaking to the same issues, when taken at face value.

The pretribulation position argued that the church would not see the wrath of God, primarily using Romans 5:9, 1 Thessalonians 1:10, 5:9, and Revelation 3:10 as their prooftexts. I had no choice but to agree because that was what the Bible clearly appeared to teach. But the position lost its biblical support when it tried to make the entire seven-year tribulation period the wrath of God, especially the intense persecution associated with the rule of Antichrist. Holding to that premise clearly contradicted other teachings of Scripture that showed the saints, the elect of God, undergoing Antichrist's persecution—the same passages of Scripture that the posttribulation Rapture position used to *prove* its position.

The posttribulation position maintained that the church will undergo the persecution of Antichrist, basing their position on several passages that clearly teach that the elect or saints of God will someday become the targets of Antichrist's persecution. Those who held to this view defended their position with passages taken from the Olivet Discourse of Christ (Matt. 24:21–22, 29–31), the second letter of Paul to the Thessalonians (2 Thess. 2:1–8), and the book of Revelation (i.e., Rev. 13:3–10; 14:9–12). I had to agree with this particular facet of posttribulationism, because when these texts were taken at face value, that was precisely what they appeared to teach.

But their position, like the pretribulation position, was not without problems. For the posttribulation view to cohere—that the Rapture will occur at the very end of the seven-year tribulation period—the position has the saints meeting Christ in the clouds and immediately returning with Him to earth at the battle of Armageddon. Here is where I had to part company with them, for there was no biblical basis to support either their specific timing of the Rapture (at the very end of the tribulation period) or their destination of the raptured and resurrected saints (back to earth rather than up into heaven). Those assumptions—which is all that they are—clearly contradicted other passages, such as those showing the elect "unblamable in holiness before our God and Father [on His throne in heaven] at the coming of our Lord Jesus with all His saints" (1 Thess. 3:13; cf. Rev. 7:9–14), and those dealing with the timing of both the Bema Seat Judgment of believers (Rev. 11:18) and the marriage of the Lamb to His bride (Rev. 19:7–9), which Christ told John would occur *in heaven* and *before* the battle of Armageddon (Rev. 19:11–21). It is difficult to place the church in heaven before the Rapture occurs on earth, to say nothing of a Rapture that never takes the church up into heaven in the first place!

In addition, the posttribulationist, unlike the pretribulationist who made the entire tribulation period the wrath of God, limited the wrath of God to an indeterminable time period at the end of the tribulation period, culminating in the battle of

Armageddon. However, their timing of the Rapture—at the very end of the tribulation period—necessitated that the church *go through* the wrath of God, a seeming contradiction to a face-value understanding of the passages we looked at earlier. In order to skirt the passages that promise believers deliverance from the wrath of God, they taught that God's wrath would fall only upon the ungodly. This, in my opinion, was stretching the point to accommodate their position.

And so the thrust of the debate centered around these two, seemingly contradictory positions. Both had their own set of references that took Scripture at face value. Both had their own set of assumptions that went beyond what they could prove biblically. And both needed to harmonize other passages that contradicted certain parts of their overall position. In other words, neither position had an airtight case capable of knocking out the opposing view, so both views continued to exist, arguing against each other but unable to adequately defend their own position.

Quotable Quotes from Those Who Know

Of course I wasn't the only one who saw the confusion that existed between the two views. One of the great proponents of the pretribulation Rapture position is Dr. John Walvoord, former president of Dallas Theological Seminary. He has written that "neither posttribulationism nor pretribulationism is an explicit teaching of the Scriptures. The Bible does not, in so many words, state either."[2]

Another advocate of the pretribulation Rapture position, a man well-respected in many conservative theological circles, is Dr. Richard Mayhue, current dean of The Master's Seminary in California. He confirms Dr. Walvoord's position, only a little more to the point. He states in his unpublished doctoral

2. John Walvoord, *The Rapture Question, 1st Ed.,* (Findlay, Ohio: n.p., 1957), 148.

dissertation, "The Prophet's Watchword, the Day of the Lord," that "neither a pretribulation nor a posttribulation Rapture is taught directly in Scripture, and pretribulationists still have problems to solve in regard to their position." He goes on to say, however, that "*perhaps* the position of pretribulationism is correct *although its proof at times has been logically invalid or at least unconvincing*" (emphasis added).[3]

To stake one's life on any doctrine that its own defenders state is "logically invalid or at least unconvincing" is too much to ask of a logical mind. I had been down a similar path with theistic evolution and vowed never to be taken in again in such a way. An issue as important as the second coming of Christ for His own, in light of the fact that His first coming was clearly and accurately predicted hundreds of times in the Old Testament, should be just as clearly taught in the New Testament.

And so, instead of looking for a single common denominator that harmonized all relevant passages without contradiction, my friends and I continued discussing the merits of these two diverse positions, with emotion, late into the night. But the debate was healthy, and as "iron sharpens iron, so one man sharpens another" (Prov. 27:17). I probably learned more about how to handle the Bible from those one-on-one debates than from any other experience in my life. A man in combat learns quickly or he dies. The best way to fight fire is with fire! So I was forced to learn, and learn I did. Later, when I began facing off with my good friend Marvin Rosenthal, all of my training with these other men would be put to the test. But that's getting ahead of the story.

Ironically, all the time we were battling over the two positions that we considered our only face-value options, the truth was there staring at us, just waiting for us to be willing to break from the traditions we had been taught and to look for the

3. Richard Mayhue, "The Prophet's Watchword, the Day of the Lord" (Ph.D. diss., Grace Theological Seminary, 1981), 181–82.

"common denominator" that made all of the passages fit perfectly together, without contradiction or inconsistency.

The Common Denominator

In the early spring of 1984, I sold my investment management company to Xerox. This freed up a tremendous amount of my time for the project at hand. Because I was working on an in-depth doctrinal statement for several ministry organizations with which I was associated, I wanted resolution on the one issue that I hadn't been able to resolve: the timing of Christ's return for His church. By now I knew all the pros and cons of both positions, but I had yet to resolve the contradictions. I agreed with Mayhue that the pretribulation position was "logically invalid or at least unconvincing," and therefore found myself leaning toward the posttribulation position because of the clear teaching of Christ in Matthew 24, the teaching of John in Revelation 12 and 13, and the teaching of Paul in 2 Thessalonians 2, all of which put the elect of God in the heart of Antichrist's persecution. But, as I mentioned earlier, there were still serious timing and destination problems associated with their position, so I refused to buy into it hook, line, and sinker.

With more of my time free for study, I went to our summer home in Michigan, taking along my computer, software that included two translations of the Bible with an exhaustive concordance, and my own thoroughly marked-up Bible. (I also took my wife, who is the best biblical sounding board a man could ever desire, as my theological friends have come to know all too well!) Sitting down at the dining room table, I then spread all the equipment and resource material out in front of me and went to work.

Because of the frequent discussions I'd had on this issue in the past, I knew right where I wanted to start: the sign that Christ refers to in His Olivet Discourse—something I'd kept coming back to again and again. Christ taught His disciples that the sign that would immediately precede the sign of His coming would be given in the sun, moon, and stars (Matt. 24:29–31). Although I had never explored the Old Testament to discover what that sign represented—who knows why?—I knew that this event was somehow the key to understanding the timing of Christ's return.

I now began the research I should have done years before. I picked up my concordance and made note of all the passages in the Bible that referred to the sun, moon, and stars together as a single unit. This research took me immediately to the Old Testament prophetic books of Isaiah, Ezekiel, and Joel. Then my study took me to the New Testament books of Matthew, Mark, and Luke, to Acts, and then to Revelation. Within a few hours of comparing Scripture with Scripture, I realized that, by God's grace, I had found the common denominator that made the biblical truths of both pretribulationism and posttribulationism come together perfectly, without contradiction, inconsistency, or unreconciled passages. In the last days, a sign will be given in the sun, moon, and stars that will initiate the Day of the Lord. When it appears in the heavenlies, the persecution of God's elect—at the hands of Antichrist—will be ended and the wrath of God against the children of Satan will begin.

How could I have missed the answer for all those years? I wondered. How had my friends and teachers missed it? Why was there so much confusion in the church at large over something so clearly revealed in Scripture? The solution was so incredibly simple!

Plain and Simple

Plainly stated, the core truth is this: *the persecution by Antichrist during the great tribulation will be the wrath of Satan* (Rev. 12:12), *not the wrath of God. When the sign of the sun, moon, and stars is given in the heavens, the wrath of Satan*

*against the elect of God will be terminated, the faithful to God
will be raptured, and then the wrath of God will begin against
the wicked who remain, ending with the battle of Armageddon.*
Thus, the Rapture of God's saints has to occur sometime during the second half of the tribulation period, during Antichrist's persecution of God's elect. Plain and simple! No more,
no less. Once you get that right, everything else falls together
perfectly! Now all I had to do was prove that this position
didn't contradict other passages in Scripture of which I might
be unaware.

I spent an incredible amount of time checking and recheck-
ing all passages that touched upon the solution I had come to.
I read all the commentaries and any other books I could get my
hands on, looking for any passage of Scripture that might contradict the conclusions I had come to believe. Eventually I became convinced that such a passage does not exist. Equally
important, I also came to realize that many of the early church
fathers—those men taught by the apostles directly, or early
church leaders one or two generations removed—who touched
on end time events in any detail at all, held to the same general
premise (that the church would undergo persecution by Antichrist) that drove the position to which I had come, with the exception of Origen and Clement of Alexandria, men whose
names have become trademarks for the mystical, allegorical
method of interpretation that I had already dismissed!

At about this same time, I was introduced to Marvin
Rosenthal, executive director of a mission to the Jews known
as Friends of Israel. Because of my love for Israel and Marvin's
charming personality, I found myself agreeing to serve on their
board of directors. But I had a problem. I couldn't sign their
statement of faith because of their strong pretribulation position. Because Marvin was responsible for putting this position
into their statement to begin with, I started a series of long-
distance conversations with him that forced me to carefully defend every jot and tittle of the new position I was taking. Every

biblical position at some time or another needs to be tried and tested by fire. Marvin became my fire.

For over a year we went back and forth, on the telephone and in person. We spent a week together on the New Jersey shore interacting with one another and with several of *his* theological friends who were either directly associated with Friends of Israel or who taught in the Bible department of Philadelphia College of the Bible. Together we examined and reexamined every passage for what it says in the light of its context. Passages that seemed to contradict each other had to be dealt with and harmonized with the whole. We argued over the meaning of the Greek, our sole intent being to find truth. No more, no less. I'd already been trained for this theological combat by virtue of the long discussions I'd had with my friends from Moody Bible Institute. They had taught me well how to defend my positions with learned men such as these, and I had a strong biblical defense for every legitimate issue raised, including those arguments that were based upon the underlying Greek text.

At the end of our long deliberations, Marvin and I stood united in what we believed, and, more important, we could defend every aspect of our position against anyone who was willing to accept Scripture at face value. No contradictory passage was buried or twisted out of context in order to make our view work. If it was truth, it would stand the heat of intense debate. It was and it did!

Now you know where I'm coming from, how I arrived at the place I am today, and why I have such confidence in the position that I present in the following pages. For lack of a better name, and to show a distinction from the pretribulation and the posttribulation positions on the Rapture, Marvin and I decided to call this view the *prewrath* Rapture position. There is nothing special or magical in the name. It is used simply to distinguish it from the other positions, but also to affirm the fact that the true child of God will be rescued from the hands of Antichrist before the wrath of God begins!

3

The Basics

Before we look at specific teachings of Christ, Paul, Peter, and John, it is necessary to understand how four distinct biblical truths are interrelated if we are to gain a proper understanding of the whole of end time events. Each of these truths plays an important part in a complete and accurate biblical view of the return of Christ, when the true children of God are raptured and the wicked who remain are destroyed.

The Wrath of God (The Day of the Lord)

The biblical teaching concerning end times primarily has to do with the judgment and wrath of God against the unrighteous world. In fact, the book of Revelation is almost entirely about God's wrath. When the angel asks, "Who is worthy to open the book and to break its seals?" (Rev. 5:2), the answer is, "the Lion that is from the tribe of Judah" (v. 5), whom John describes to his readers as "a Lamb" (v. 6), a reference to Jesus Christ.

Christ came the first time as the Lamb of God to pay the price for sin. When He comes the second time, it will be as the Lion of Judah to judge human-

51

kind. In those days, only Christ will be worthy to break the seals and open the scroll because God "has fixed a day in which He will judge the world in righteousness through a Man [Christ] whom He has appointed, having furnished proof to all men by raising Him from the dead" (Acts 17:31; cf. John 5:22, 27, 30).

In the last days, the wrath of God will be played out during a specific time period called *the Day of the Lord*. There are frequent Old and New Testament references to this day of God's judgment against the wicked, but the Old Testament is where this great day of God's wrath is first explained.

The Hebrew word for day (*yôm*) can mean a twenty-four-hour day if used with a specific number or with other specific time language such as morning and evening, as in the case with the creation account recorded in Genesis 1. *Yôm* also can be used to describe a longer time frame, such as that referred to by the prophet Isaiah when he wrote about the millennial rule of Messiah: "In that *day* the Branch of the LORD [Christ] will be beautiful and glorious, and the fruit of the earth will be the pride and the adornment of the survivors of Israel" (Isa. 4:2, emphasis added; cf. Hos. 1:11). In this instance, day clearly refers to a longer time frame than just one twenty-four-hour day.

The latter is also true of the Day of the Lord. It will be a time period of unknown duration when God destroys the wicked inhabitants living upon earth. However, there are several specific things we do know about that day.

The prophet Isaiah teaches us that during the Day of the Lord, "the pride of man will be humbled, and the loftiness of men will be abased, and *the LORD alone will be exalted in that day*" (Isa. 2:17, emphasis added). The critical teaching of this passage is that *the LORD alone will be exalted during His day*. Remember that. It's important! We will deal with this concept more thoroughly in the third point dealing with the wrath of Satan.

Zephaniah tells us that during the Day of the Lord "all the earth will be devoured in the fire of His jealousy, for He will make a complete end, indeed a terrifying one, of all the inhabitants of the earth" (Zeph. 1:18). The apostle John tells us that the Day of the Lord will be a time of God's wrath: "'Fall on us and hide us from the presence of Him who sits on the throne, and from the *wrath of the Lamb; for the great day of their wrath has come;* and who is able to stand?'" (Rev. 6:16–17, emphasis added). Peter picks up the same theme, saying, "But the present heavens and earth by His word are being *reserved for fire, kept for the day of judgment and destruction of ungodly men*. . . . But the day of the Lord will come like a thief, in which the heavens will pass away with a roar and the elements will be destroyed with intense heat, and the earth and its works will be burned up" (2 Pet. 3:7, 10, emphasis added). And so, we see that the Day of the Lord is a day of judgment—of *fiery* judgment—a day when God unleashes His wrath against the wicked living on earth.

Next, it is very important to remember the terminology that Christ uses to refer to His great day of judgment. *When Christ speaks of "the end of the age" or just simply, "the end," He is referring to the Day of the Lord.* Explaining to His disciples the meaning of the wheat and tare parable, Christ tells them that "the harvest is the end of the age; and the reapers are angels. Therefore *just as the tares are gathered up and burned with fire, so shall it be at the end of the age*" (Matt. 13:39–40, emphasis added).

One important word of explanation needs to be made here. Often, when explaining the totality of the destruction of the Day of the Lord upon humankind, I am asked: "Who, then, is left upon earth to become the citizens of the Millennial Kingdom ruled by Christ?" The answer is as simple as it is biblical. The primary inhabitants of the Millennial Kingdom will be the remnant of the nation of Israel who survive the final seven-year tribulation period. There will be 144,000 Jews who become the "firstfruits" of Israel unto Christ, saved right when the Rapture occurs sometime during the second three-and-a-half years of the tribulation period; these will be sealed in their foreheads for their protection when the Day of the Lord begins, the time of God's wrath that immediately follows their salvation (Rev. 7:3–8; cf. 14:4). The rest of the nation of Israel who survive this seven-year tribulation period (Isa. 4:2) will likewise become true children of God, but not until after the tribulation period is complete, after "the fulness of the Gentiles has come in" (Rom. 11:25–26; cf. Luke 21:24), when "everlasting righteousness" will be brought in to the nation of Israel (Dan. 9:24).

So remember, when reference is made to "the end" or to "the end of the age," it is a reference to the Day of the Lord, a prolonged period of time when the fiery wrath of God will be poured out upon all who remain on earth after the righteous have been raptured. For "the Lord knows how to rescue the godly from temptation [testing], and to keep the unrighteous under punishment for the day of judgment" (2 Pet. 2:9). But, even more important, it will be a time when God and God alone will be exalted!

The Sign of the Day of the Lord

Because of the severity of the Day of the Lord, God has promised to first give the world a sign in the heavens announcing that the day of His wrath is about to begin. The Old Testament book of Joel is devoted almost entirely to the Day of the Lord, and in it the prophet explains that God "will display wonders in the sky and on the earth. . . . The sun will be turned into darkness, and the moon into blood, *before* the great and awesome day of the LORD comes" (2:30–31, emphasis added). In the following chapter he again refers to the sign that will announce this great day of God's wrath: "The sun and moon grow dark, and the stars lose their brightness. And the LORD roars from Zion" (3:15–16).

The final book of the Bible, the book of Revelation (in particular 6:16–17), also predicts this sign given in the sun, moon, and stars as a precursor to the Day of the Lord. In his vision on the island of Patmos, the apostle John saw that at the opening of the sixth seal,

(12) there was a great earthquake; and the sun became black as sackcloth made of hair, and the whole moon became like blood; (13) and the stars of the sky fell to the earth. . . . (14) And the sky was split apart like a scroll when it is rolled up; and every mountain and island were moved out of their places. (15) And the kings of the earth and the great men and the commanders and the rich and the strong and every slave and free man, hid themselves in the caves and among the rocks of the mountains; (16) and they said to the mountains and to the rocks, "Fall on us and hide us from the presence of Him who sits on the throne, and from the wrath of the Lamb; (17) for the great day of their wrath has come; and who is able to stand?" (Rev. 6:12–17).

When the sign of the sun, moon, and stars is given in the heavens, the whole world will be terrified. On the other hand, the reaction of the saints of God will be just the opposite! Christ instructed His disciples that

(25) "there will be *signs in sun and moon and stars,* and upon the earth dismay among nations, in perplexity at the roaring of the sea and the waves, (26) *men fainting from fear and the expectation of the things which are coming upon the world.* . . . (28) But [elect of God] when these things begin to take place, straighten up and *lift up your heads, because your redemption* [your release, previously paid for] *is drawing near*" (Luke 21:25–26, 28, emphasis added).

Is it any wonder, then, that Peter, referring to the Day of the Lord, says to genuine believers: "Since all these things are to be destroyed in this way, what sort of people ought you to be in holy conduct and godliness, looking for and hastening the coming of the day of God . . ." (2 Pet. 3:11–12a)?

As I mentioned in the previous chapter, I have carefully studied every biblical passage in which the diminished light of the sun, moon, and stars is mentioned in conjunction with one another. In *every* case it refers to the same thing: the sign that God has promised to give just prior to unleashing His wrath upon the unrighteous. With this in mind, it is interesting to note that in Genesis 1 we are told that "God said, 'Let there be lights in the expanse of the heavens to separate the day from the night, and let them be for *signs*, and for seasons, and for days and years'" (1:14, emphasis added).

One purpose of the sun, moon, and stars is to be "lights in the expanse of the heavens" to serve as a sign. A sign of what? As we shall see in more detail in the next chapter, it is a sign that will be given just preceding the coming of Christ. It is also a sign that will announce the Day of the Lord—the wrath of God at the end of the age.

A star in the east announced the first coming of Christ, when He came as a Lamb (Matt. 2:9–10). The sun, moon, and stars will announce His second coming, when He comes as a Lion (Matt. 24:29–30; cf. Rev. 6:12–17).

The Wrath of Satan

This perhaps is the most important of the four truths to understand and remember, for the persecution of the elect associated with Antichrist is not the wrath of *God;* it is the wrath of *Satan.* As we saw earlier in this chapter, the wrath of God is, by definition, against the wicked, when *"the LORD alone will be exalted"* (Isa. 2:17, emphasis added). Likewise, as we shall see, the converse is true. The wrath of Satan will be against the righteous children of God, when the powerful minion of Satan, Antichrist, *"exalts himself above every so-called god* or object of worship, so that he takes his seat in the temple of God, displaying himself as being God" (2 Thess. 2:4, emphasis added).

Unless you separate the wrath of God (when the Lord alone will be exalted) from the persecution associated with Antichrist (when Antichrist will exalt himself above every so-called god, demanding the worship of the world and killing those who don't comply), you have a very serious contradiction. And when you have contradictions, you don't have truth! The only way these two passages can be harmonized is to realize that Antichrist's persecution of God's elect cannot be equated with the wrath of God against the wicked.

Scripture clearly teaches that Antichrist's persecution will be against the elect of God (Matt. 24:21–22), against His saints (Rev. 13:7), against those "who keep the commandments of God and hold to the testimony of Jesus" (Rev. 12:17)! On the other hand, Scripture is just as clear that the wrath of God is against "ungodly men" (2 Pet. 3:7) "because they have sinned against the LORD; and their blood will be poured out like dust, and their flesh like dung. Neither their silver nor their gold will be able to deliver them on the Day of the LORD's wrath; and all the earth will be devoured in the fire of His jealousy, for He will make a complete end, indeed a terrifying one, of all the inhabitants of the earth" (Zeph. 1:17b–18).

Do we dare put the elect of God, whether they live *before or after* the beginning of the seven-year-tribulation period, on the receiving end of His great wrath? To do so we make God responsible for Antichrist's persecution of those who will stand true to Christ during this terrible time of testing. May it never be! Our Lord has already promised His children that they will not see the wrath of God (Rom. 5:9; 1 Thess. 1:10; 5:9). *That promise applies to all the elect of God, not just to those who are living before the final seven-year tribulation period!* Just the opposite is true: God's righteous wrath will be against the unrighteous, the children of Satan who have been persecuting the children of God.

And so the question: Who or what is responsible for the persecution of God's children at the hands of Antichrist? The answer is given us in the book of Revelation, where John is told to tell his readers:

> (12) "Woe to the earth and the sea, because *the devil has come down to you, having great wrath,* knowing that he has only a short time. . . ." (4) and [the whole earth] *worshiped the dragon* [Satan], *because he gave his authority to the beast* [Antichrist]; and *they worshiped the beast.* . . . (5) and authority to act for forty-two months was given to him [Antichrist]. . . . (7) *And it was given to him* [Antichrist] *to make war with the saints and to overcome them* (Rev. 12:12; 13:4, 5, 7a, emphasis added).

The "who" is Satan; the "what" is his wrath; the "when" is during the great tribulation—that is, the final forty-two months of the tribulation period. Put together, Antichrist's persecution of God's elect is the wrath of Satan! Plain and simple.

It is God's wrath that will bring Satan's wrath to an end, when God rescues His faithful children from Antichrist's persecution and then begins His destruction of the wicked who remain. Paul put it this way:

> (6) For after all it is only just for God to repay with affliction those who afflict you [persecution at the hands of Antichrist], (7) and to give relief to you who are afflicted and to us as well [the rapture of the saints] when the Lord Jesus shall be revealed from heaven with His mighty angels in flaming fire, (8) dealing out retribution to those who do not know God and to those who do not obey the gospel of our Lord Jesus [the Day of the Lord]" (2 Thess. 1:6–8).

The Rapture Initiates God's Wrath— on the Same Day

The Rapture will occur on the very day that God's wrath begins. How do we know? From the teaching of Christ. He said,

(22) "The days shall come when you will long to see one of the days of the Son of Man, and you will not see it. . . . (26) And just as it happened in the days of Noah, so it shall be also in the days of the Son of Man: (27) they were eating, they were drinking, they were marrying, they were being given in marriage, until *the day that Noah entered the ark, and the flood came and destroyed them all.* (28) It was the same as happened in the days of Lot: they were eating, they were drinking, they were buying, they were selling, they were planting, they were building; (29) *but on the day that Lot went out from Sodom it rained fire and brimstone from heaven and destroyed them all.* (30) *It will be just the same on the day that the Son of Man is revealed*" (Luke 17:22, 26–30, emphasis added).

On the day that the Son of Man is revealed, Christ says, it will be just as it was in the days of Noah and Lot. God will deliver His faithful from persecution and then, on the same day, begin His destruction of the wicked who remain.

Why, you may ask, is that so important? For several reasons. First, in the next chapter when we begin our study of the passages that clearly give us the timing of the rapture of the saints, we will see that these same two events—the Rapture and God's wrath—are tied together. That will be the case in every passage we look at that deals with the timing of the Rapture. So it is important to understand that Christ taught that these two back-to-back events would occur *on the same day.*

Second, if these two events do occur on the same day, the idea of the *imminent* return of Christ as defined by the pretribulation Rapturists—the very heart of the pretribulation Rapture position—is destroyed. According to their view of imminency, the rapture of God's elect could occur at "any moment." Prophetically, they argue, nothing has had to occur since Christ's ascension recorded in Acts 1:9–11. However, if the Rapture does initiate the wrath of God *on the same day,* then the doctrine of imminency as defined above is demolished, since important events need to occur *prior to* the beginning of the Day of the Lord.[1] The wrath of God in the last days will be against Antichrist and the unrighteous inhabitants and armies of his earthly kingdom. Therefore, if the Rapture occurs on the same day the wrath begins, Antichrist *must* already be on the scene and Israel *must* be back in her own homeland (Dan. 9:24, 27), making the Rapture impossible for the past two thousand years, right up until 1948, when Israel once again became a sovereign nation.

Thus, because of the problems associated with having these two great end time events occur (or begin) on the same day, those holding to the pretribulation Rapture position will appeal to the Flood story recorded in Genesis 7 in their attempt to explain away the words of Christ quoted above. Here God commanded Noah:

(1) "Enter the ark, you and all your household; for you alone I have seen to be righteous before Me in this time. (2) You shall take with you of every clean animal by sevens, a male and his

---

1. It is upon the translation of eight separate Greek words into English that the "any moment" return of Christ is built. In the NAS, *prosdechomai* is translated "looking for"; *apekdechomai* is translated "waiting for," "waiting eagerly," or "eagerly await"; *ekdechomai*, "waits for"; *prosdokaō*, "expect" or "looking for"; *grēgoreō*, "alert" or "awake"; *agrupneō*, "alert"; *anamenō*, "wait"; and *eggizō*, "near" or "at hand." *Without a single exception, none of these Greek words have the core meaning of imminency*—that Christ's return could occur at any moment. Each of these particular Greek words, except one, deals with the *believer's attitude concerning Christ's return—one of expectancy—not the timing of His coming*.

The one exception is the Greek word *eggizō*, translated in James 5:8 as "at hand." More specifically, the word means "to be near" or "to approach" with regard to either time or space. It has nothing to do with an "any moment" occurrence of the subject matter being addressed. This specific word was commonly used in connection with approaching feasts, such as Passover, Tabernacles, and so on (see John 2:13; 7:2; 11:55), and although the Jewish holiday was near or approaching, the time affixed for the Jewish feast was never imminent. The day and time of these Jewish holidays were rigorously governed by calendric regulations, set in concrete by Jewish law.

In James 5:8–9, *eggizō* is referring to Christ's personal closeness (*parousía* can be translated "coming" or "presence," depending on the context), during times of great distress. It is intended to be an encouragement to righteous men who have been condemned or treated unfairly by wicked men (vv. 4, 6), exhorting them to be patient (vv. 7, 8), to endure (v. 11), for their suffering will be avenged: "the *Judge* [of those persecuting you] stands right before the doors" (v. 9).

female; and of the animals that are not clean two, a male and his female. . . . (4) For after seven more days, I will send rain on the earth forty days and forty nights; and I will blot out from the face of the land every living thing that I have made" (Gen. 7:1–2, 4).

Pretribulationists appeal to the phrase, "after seven more days, I will send rain on the earth." They argue that Noah and his family entered the ark seven days before the rains began, rather than understanding the passage to mean that Noah had seven more days to gather the animals together, after which he and his family were to enter the ark and the rains would begin. Taking that second option might harmonize the words of Christ with the Flood account recorded in Genesis, but it would destroy their doctrine of imminency! Instead, to protect their position on the imminent return of Christ, they must take the first option even though it directly contradicts the words of Christ in Luke 17. Thus, they will tell you the rapture of the church parallels Noah's entrance into the safety of the ark, and that the rains that fell seven days later parallel the wrath of God in the last days, the tribulation period. By separating the time Noah entered the ark from the beginning of the rains, pretribulationists maintain that the Rapture could occur "any moment" and the other events that need to be in place before the tribulation period can begin—that is, Israel's return to the land and the appearance of Antichrist—could or would occur in the time frame represented by the seven-day delay Noah had, sitting in the ark!

Granted, a face-value understanding of verse 4 alone does not tell us for certain whether Noah entered the ark seven days before the flood rains began or on the same day. But when we compare Scripture with Scripture, the words of Christ tell us that these two events *did* occur on the same day. So, although two options may exist when looking at verse 4 alone, there can be only one valid interpretation of this verse when Scripture is compared with Scripture—the way Christ explains it!

Yet there are still some who would rather challenge the statement of Christ than yield on this point that makes their concept of *imminency* impossible. They adamantly teach that Noah entered the ark seven days before the rains came, disregarding the clear teaching of Christ in Luke 17. For example, Dr. John A. McLean, in an article printed in Dallas Theological Seminary's scholastic quarterly *Bibliotheca Sacra*, maintains that the "argument of a 'same day' rapture with the Day of the Lord *does not stand up to biblical scrutiny*. After Noah's family and the animals entered the Ark, the Flood waters *did not begin for seven days* (Gen. 7:7, 10)."[2] In other words, when Christ told His disciples that both of these events would occur on the same day, He was wrong. Had Christ forgotten that Noah had entered the ark seven days in advance of the flood rains? Was Christ trying to deceive His disciples? Was Christ just confused? Of course not!

Looking carefully at the context of the account recorded in Genesis 7, we discover that the Flood passage does not end at verse 10 as Dr. McLean would have the reader believe. Instead, it goes on to explain that

(11) In the six hundredth year of Noah's life, in the second month, on the seventeenth day of the month, *on the same day* all the fountains of the great deep burst open, and the floodgates of the sky were opened. (12) And the rain fell upon the earth for forty days and forty nights. (13) *On the very same day Noah and Shem and Ham and Japheth, the sons of Noah, and Noah's wife and the three wives of his sons with them, entered the ark* (Gen. 7:11–13, emphasis added).

In other words, the instruction Christ gives His disciples concerning the interval between the Rapture of the church and

2. John A. McLean, *Bibliotheca Sacra* (October–December 1991), 394.

the beginning of God's wrath upon those who remain is identical to the Genesis account of the Flood, when taken in its entirety. The context from which our text-in-question is derived clearly shows that "*on the very same day* Noah . . . entered the ark," "the fountains of the great deep burst open, and the floodgates of the sky were opened" (Gen. 7:13, 11). "It will be just the same," Jesus said, "*on the day* that the Son of Man is revealed" (Luke 17:30).

Why, then, does a face-value understanding of what Christ taught "not stand up to biblical scrutiny," to use the language of Dr. McLean? And who, then, is playing games with the text? Here we plainly see an example of blatant twisting of a text to defend a position whose "proof at times has been logically invalid or at least unconvincing," to use the language of Dr. Mayhue.

Notice how Peter makes the same argument, using the same parallel as Christ and putting the same two events—the Rapture and God's wrath—side by side. In fact, he is even more precise in the language he uses.

> (4) For if God did not spare . . . (5) the ancient world, but preserved Noah, a preacher of righteousness, with seven others, when He brought a flood upon the world of the ungodly . . . (9) then the Lord knows how to rescue [rapture] the godly from temptation [testing—Antichrist's persecution], and to keep the unrighteous under punishment for the day of judgment [the Day of the Lord] (2 Pet. 2:4–5, 9).

And the apostle Paul, referring to the same two events, tells us specifically *when* those who are being afflicted by Antichrist's persecution will be given their relief:

> (6) For after all it is only just for God to repay with affliction those who afflict you (7) and to give relief to you who are afflicted and to us as well when the Lord Jesus shall be revealed from heaven with His mighty angels in flaming fire, (8) dealing

out retribution to those who do not know God and to whose who
do not obey the gospel of our Lord Jesus (2 Thess. 1:6–8, emphasis added).

The true children of God will be given relief from their affliction *when* the day of the Lord's wrath comes, "when the
Lord Jesus shall be revealed from heaven with His mighty angels in flaming fire." Not one moment earlier, not seven years
earlier, but on the same day, at that precise moment!

In the chapters that follow we will look more closely at the
specific passages of Scripture that most clearly teach the timing of Christ's return for His church. And we will see, again
and again, that the Rapture always triggers God's wrath. These
two back-to-back events are inseparably interconnected and
are played out together in every passage we will study.

Summing It Up

Let me close this chapter by summarizing the conclusions
we have reached thus far. First, the wrath of God that will be
poured out upon the wicked in end times is called "the Day of
the Lord," "the end," or "the end of the age." This will be an
extended period of time when God, not Antichrist, "alone will
be exalted," when He will systematically destroy the unrighteous who remain on earth after the faithful have been removed.

Second, the wrath of God will immediately follow a sign that
He will give in the heavens—in the sun, moon, and stars—
warning the world of what is to follow, and telling the saints of
God to look up because the time for their deliverance has
come.

Third, the wrath of God should never be confused with the
wrath of Satan, who is the power behind Antichrist's persecution of God's elect. Antichrist alone will be exalted in his day,
during the wrath of Satan against the children of God. The

Lord alone will be exalted during His day, during the wrath of God against the children of Satan! Although the saints will undergo the wrath of Satan, they will never undergo the wrath of God!

Therefore, the fourth point to remember is that "on the day that the Son of Man is revealed" the saints will be rescued and God's wrath will begin against those who remain . . . as it was in the days of Noah, as it was in the days of Lot. The elect of God will be rescued from the wrath of Satan (at the hands of Antichrist) on the very day the wrath of God begins!

Now, using what we have established in the three previous chapters, we will begin to look more specifically at what the Scriptures have to say about the timing of Christ's return for His church—in particular, the teachings of Christ, Paul, Peter, and John—faithfully following the face-value hermeneutic we learned in chapter 1. Plain and simple.

4

The Teaching of Christ

Christ's Olivet Discourse (Matt. 24:3–25:46; cf. Mark 13:3–37) is the most critical of all the New Testament writings concerning the timing of when Christ will come to rescue the elect and destroy the wicked who remain. In this end time instruction by Christ, He specifically teaches His disciples concerning the sign of His coming and of the end of the age. It is a compact overview of the things that will occur in the last days.

In this discourse, Christ refers His disciples back to the Old Testament book of Daniel where, in chapter 10, a heavenly messenger gives Daniel an amazing prophecy concerning the last days which the prophet then records in chapters 11–12. Included in this critical passage is the time frame within which end time events will be played out.

Taken in tandem with the Olivet Discourse, the book of Revelation—the revelation of Christ, written to His bond-servants—fills in the details concerning end time events, rounding out this critical trilogy that deals with the last days. And when the heavenly messenger in Daniel 10 is compared carefully to the description of Christ in Revelation 1, we quickly see that they are one and the same person.

Thus, it is Christ Himself who is responsible for giving His saints the most specific and significant prophecy concerning the end times—including an overview of these events in the Olivet Discourse, the time frame in which these events will occur in the book of Daniel, and the details concerning these events in the book of Revelation. When these three end time passages are compared to one another—which we will do together in the following chapters—their symmetry and harmony become obvious. But of the three, the account most critical to our understanding of the timing of Christ's return is given us in the Olivet Discourse, as recorded in Matthew 24, because it deals with two back-to-back, end time events—the Rapture and God's wrath—and precisely when these events will occur in relation to the time of Antichrist's persecution, which, of course, is a focal point of all end time debates.

The Context

Christ gave this discourse to His disciples on the Mount of Olives during the final week of His earthly life. Only a few days earlier, on His way to Jerusalem for this final time, the Lord had told His disciples,

> (18) "Behold, we are going up to Jerusalem; and the Son of Man will be delivered to the chief priests and scribes, and they will condemn Him to death, (19) and will deliver Him to the Gentiles to mock and scourge and crucify Him, and on the third day He will be raised up" (**MATT. 20:18–19**).

Now, on the day after Christ's triumphal entry into Jerusalem, He and His disciples went up to the temple. After Jesus contended verbally with the Jewish religious leaders, someone close to where He stood commented on the beauty of the temple, adorned as it was with such beautiful stones. Responding to the remark, Jesus turned to His disciples and told them that "the days will come in which there will not be left one stone upon another which will not be torn down" (Luke 21:6).

The disciples asked: "Teacher, when therefore will these things be?" (v. 7).

At that time, while still inside the temple, Christ answered the disciples' question. He explained to them that the day was coming when this magnificent temple would be destroyed and that Jerusalem would "be trampled underfoot . . . until the times of the Gentiles be fulfilled" (v. 24). They were not to be misled (v. 8). All these things must occur before the sign would be given in the "sun and moon and stars" (v. 25), and "the Son of Man [would be seen] coming in a cloud with power and great glory" (v. 27)!

The Question

Later that same day, Christ and His disciples left the temple and crossed the Kidron Valley to the Mount of Olives. I have to believe that, at that point, their thoughts must have been racing. Soon, they knew, Christ must die. Their leader would be gone! They had also been told that their magnificent temple would be destroyed, not one stone left upon another, and Jerusalem would continue to be trampled underfoot until the times of the Gentiles were fulfilled. That was the bad news. But Christ had also told them He was going to return. When the sign was given in the sun, moon, and stars, they would see Him coming in the clouds, with power and great glory! Now, they wanted to know only one thing: *When?!*

> And as He [Christ] was sitting on the Mount of Olives, the disciples came to Him privately, saying, "Tell us, when will these things be, and what will be the sign of Your coming, and of the end of the age?" (MATT. 24:3).

As we saw in the previous chapter, Jesus had already taught His disciples that His return would be connected with the judgment of God that would occur at "the end of the age." Both of these events—His coming and His judgment—would occur on the same day. Thus, their question to Christ tied the two events together, as it should have. What they did not yet know was *what* the sign of these two back-to-back events would be, or *when*, precisely, they would occur. Therefore they asked Him, "What will be the sign of Your coming and of the end of the age?"

The Overview

It is within this context that Christ began His Olivet Discourse, answering His disciples' questions by first giving them an overview of end time events. After the death and resurrection of their Lord, these loyal but now bewildered men would become the founding fathers of the church. As such, Christ needed to instruct them carefully concerning His return, for that glorious event would, understandably, become the great hope of the church (Titus 2:13). For that reason, the first thing He said was

"See to it that no one misleads you" (**MATT. 24:4**).

Then, in the context of this warning, Christ gave His disciples a general overview of the events that will occur in the last days (Matt. 24:5–14), leading right up to His coming and to the deliverance of His elect, after which "the end shall come" (v. 14).

(5) "For many will come in My name, saying, 'I am the Christ' and will mislead many. (6) And you will be hearing of wars and rumors of wars; see that you are not frightened, for those things must take place, but that is not yet the end. (7) For nation will rise against nation, and kingdom against kingdom, and in various places there will be famines and earthquakes. (8) But all these things are merely the beginning of birth pangs" (**MATT. 24:5–8**).

In the last days, certain clear signposts will inform the elect of God that Christ's coming is approaching. First there will be false Christs; then there will be wars and rumors of wars (vv. 5–6a). But, He warned, those worldwide events should not be confused with the wrath of God, because the end of the age—when God's wrath will destroy the wicked by fire—is still future (v. 6b). Christ tells His disciples in verse 6, "those things must take place, but that is not yet the end."

The wars will be followed by famines and earthquakes (v. 7), but all of those terrible things are "merely the beginning of birth pangs" (v. 8). That phrase is the graphic comparison Christ used to explain that as difficult as the "beginning birth pangs" may seem, they will be mild compared to the "hard labor," so to speak, that immediately follows.

Then He explained to His disciples what that "hard labor" will be.

"Then they will deliver you to tribulation, and will kill you, and you will be hated by all nations on account of My name" (**MATT. 24:9**).[1]

Notice those who will be affected by the persecution—the "hard labor" that follows the "beginning birth pangs." The persecution will not be against the world (*they*), but against the true children of God (*you*)! *They* will be the ones who deliver *you* and kill *you* and hate *you*. Why? "On account of My

1. The Greek word *thlípsis*, which is here translated "tribulation," can also be translated "persecution," as is done in Acts 11:19. I personally think "persecution" gives the reader a better understanding of what is occurring, when taken in the context of Matt. 24:21–22, "for then there will be a great tribulation [*thlípsis*], such as has not occurred since the beginning of the world. . . . And unless those days had been cut short, no life would have been saved; but for the sake of the elect those days shall be cut short." Obviously, from the context of our passage, this time of great tribulation is not a time of tribulation against the world in general, but a time of tribulation targeted specifically against the elect of God and any others who refuse to worship Antichrist (i.e., a time of great persecution; see Rev. 12:9–13:10).

name," because of *your* open identification with Christ. That will be the hard labor that *follows* the beginning birth pangs.

In the parallel account of the Olivet Discourse recorded by Mark, the true child of God undergoing this time of persecution is promised help: "'And when they arrest *you* and deliver *you* up, do not be anxious beforehand about what *you* are to say, but say whatever is given *you* in that hour; for it is not *you* who speak, but it is the Holy Spirit'" (Mark 13:11, emphasis added).

Again, the personal pronoun identifies those the Spirit will help during this terrible time of persecution. *You! Thus, it becomes apparent that the beginning birth pangs will affect everyone in the world, including those who profess the name of Christ, but the time of tribulation against you—the hard labor so to speak—will primarily affect only those who truly honor the name of Christ. You!* For this reason the Holy Spirit's special presence is promised to the elect of God during this terrible time of persecution.

The verses that immediately follow the introduction of the hard labor theme are, perhaps, some of the saddest verses in the entire Bible. Look at what will happen when *you* who profess Christ are put to the test "on account of My name" during this terrible time of persecution:

(10) "And at that time many will fall away and will deliver up one another and hate one another. (11) And many false prophets will arise, and will mislead many. (12) And because lawlessness is increased, most people's love [for Christ] will grow cold" (**MATT.** 24:10–12).[2]

---

2. This will be a very specific falling away that will occur in the last days. The Greek word behind "fall away" is *skandalízō*, a very powerful term. Its original meaning was "to be ensnared, as in a trap." Although it has a wide variety of uses, the one that is best for this context is the idea of *cowering away in shame*. The verb is passive, which means that the subject is caught in a position that leads to a denial of Christ.

The immediate context of those who "fall away" and those whose "love will grow cold" are those who will be threatened by persecution "on account of My name."

Thus, because *you* (who claim the name of Christ) will face hatred and death on account of that name, many professing Christians will fall away from the faith. Others' love for Christ will grow cold. Is it any wonder, then, that John calls this time of intense persecution "the hour of testing, that hour which is about to come upon the whole world to test those who dwell upon the earth" (Rev. 3:10)? Is it any wonder that Paul refers to this time when "many will fall away," as "*the* apostasy" (2 Thess. 2:3, emphasis added)? Or that we are asked by John, "Who is the liar but the one who denies that Jesus is the Christ?" and then are told to "abide in Him, so that when He appears, we may have confidence and not shrink away from Him in shame at His coming" (1 John 2:22a, 28)?

On their final journey together to Jerusalem, in the context of Luke 17, where Christ had just explained that the righteous would be rescued on the same day God's wrath began, Christ asked the disciples, "Shall not God bring about justice for His elect [undergoing persecution], who cry to Him day and night, and will He delay long over [coming to rescue] them? I tell you that He will bring justice [God's wrath] for them speedily. *However, when the Son of Man comes, will He find faith on the earth?*" (Luke 18:7–8, emphasis added).

A powerful question, and one that is particularly frightening in light of this great apostasy Christ foretells will occur when the church is put to the test, just before He comes to rescue the overcomers who have remained faithful to Him (see the frequent references to overcomers in Rev. 2–3).

However, later in the Olivet Discourse Christ answers His own question when He tells His disciples that no matter how bad the apostasy of professing Christians will be, some will stay true to Him, right up until the very end. To these faithful overcomers He then gives this promise:

"But the one who endures to the end [of the age, the Day of the Lord], he shall be saved [delivered]" (**MATT. 24:13**).[3]

Those who remain faithful to Christ will be delivered from this terrible time of tribulation—when "they . . . will kill you . . . and you will be hated"—and then the end of the age, God's wrath, will come. First, Satan's persecution of God's elect; then, God rescues His faithful; then, God destroys the wicked who remain, plain and simple.

Peter is even more precise in the language he uses. Referring to those who will endure Antichrist's persecution until the end, Peter promises that "the Lord knows how to *rescue* the godly from temptation [testing], and to keep the unrighteous under punishment for the day of judgment" (2 Pet. 2:9, emphasis added).[4] Once again, God rescues His faithful from testing, then destroys the wicked who remain!

Returning now to the Olivet Discourse, we see that Christ goes on to state that

"this gospel of the kingdom shall be preached in the whole world for a witness to all the nations, and then the end [of the age] shall come" (**MATT. 24:14**).

Completing the overview of end time events, Christ tells His disciples that *only after* the gospel is preached to all nations, "then the end shall come." In light of this condi-

3. The Greek word *sōthēsetai,* here translated "saved," has a wide variety of meanings that range from spiritual salvation to physical deliverance. In this context, Christ is referring to genuine Christians who will endure the persecution right up until the end of the age. By definition, they must already have been spiritually saved. Therefore, the word in this context must refer to their physical deliverance, when God rescues (or raptures) the righteous out from the midst of this great time of persecution, after which the end of the age will come.

4. The Greek verb *rhúomai,* here translated "rescue," refers to deliverance from trouble. It is used in Matt. 27:43, when the bystanders at the cross taunted Christ and said, "He trusts in God; let Him [God] *deliver* Him [Christ] now. . . ." It is also the same word found in 1 Thess. 1:10, referring to "Jesus, who *delivers* us from the wrath to come."

tion, later, after His resurrection, Christ gives His disciples—soon to be the founding fathers of the church—their Great Commission to evangelize the world. (More will be said about the Great Commission in the next chapter.)

There has been great confusion concerning verse 14, which states that the end of the age—when those who have endured are delivered or rescued—cannot occur until the whole world has heard the gospel of Christ. In fact, this verse has been the driving force behind many mission agencies who sincerely believe that by their combined missionary efforts they will usher in the Millennial Kingdom of Christ, in effect forcing end time events by worldwide propagation of the gospel.

I am not so sure that the church can or will ever accomplish this lofty goal. But *God* can and *God* will. Despite the disobedience and weakness of His own people, God will fulfill His Word on His own timetable (see Isa. 46:9–11). And by comparing Scripture with Scripture, we find out how.

When this time of great tribulation begins, John was shown

(16) another angel flying in midheaven, having an eternal gospel to preach to those who live on the earth, and to every nation and tribe and tongue and people; (17) and he said with a loud voice, "Fear God, and give Him glory, because the hour of His judgment [the end of the age, the Day of the Lord] has come" (Rev. 14:6–7).

Thus, through this worldwide angelic messenger and message, every man, woman, and child will have heard the gospel of Christ before God rescues His saints and destroys the wicked at the end of the age. Regardless of how effective or ineffective our missionary effort may be, God's own angelic messenger will preach the gospel to every nation and tribe and tongue and people, "and then the end shall come" (Matt. 24:14).

Christ's general overview of the end time events that will occur in connection with the seven-year tribulation period,

ends at Matthew 24:14. Remember the important sequence
that He has just given His disciples.

First, the false Christs (v. 5),

then the wars and rumors of wars (v. 6a), but "the end"
(God's wrath) is still to come (v. 6b).

Next will come famines and earthquakes (v. 7), but all of
these things are merely beginning birth pangs (v. 8) in comparison to the hard labor that will soon follow.

Then the hard labor will begin, when they will "kill you and
you will be hated by all nations on account of My name" (v. 9).

Then many will fall away from their faith in Christ (v. 10),
and most people's love for Christ will grow cold (v. 12).

But those who endure to "the end" (v. 13) will *then* be delivered, although not until *after* all humankind is given one last
chance to respond to the gospel (v. 14a).

Then—on the same day the elect are delivered—"the end"
(God's wrath) will come (v. 14b).

In other words, the wrath of God—the end—will not come
until *after* the beginning birth pangs, until *after* the hard labor
associated with Antichrist begins, until *after* the whole world
has been given one last chance, until *after* the deliverance of
the faithful . . . "and then the end shall come." Or, from a different perspective, first the beginning birth pangs, then the
hard labor, then delivery. Those of you who are parents, especially you mothers, can remember that sequence!

Does Christ teach that God's elect will undergo Antichrist's
persecution? Absolutely! He states this unequivocally in verse
9, when compared to the remainder of the Olivet Discourse, in
particular verses 21 and 22, which we will look at next.

Does Christ teach that Antichrist's persecution is the wrath
of God? No! In fact, quite the opposite! In verses 12 and 13
Christ teaches that the end of the age (the wrath of God) cannot occur until *after* those who endure the tribulation are first
delivered.

Does Christ teach that God's elect will undergo the wrath of God when the end of the age begins? No! Again, Christ tells us just the opposite! He makes it clear in verses 13 and 14 that those who endure this persecution at the hands of Antichrist will be delivered *before* the end—God's wrath—will come.

Survival Information

Beginning in Matthew 24:15, Christ shifts from general overview to specific information; this shift is indicated by the word *therefore*. Here, He begins to give His disciples information that those going into the perilous last days will need to know in order to survive.

> (15) "Therefore, *when you see the Abomination of Desolation* which was spoken of through Daniel the prophet, *standing in the holy place* . . . (21) *then there will be a great tribulation* [or persecution], such as has not occurred since the beginning of the world until now, nor ever shall. (22) And unless those days had been cut short, no life would have been saved; *but for the sake of the elect those days shall be cut short*" (**MATT. 24:15, 21–22**, emphasis added).

For the first time in the recorded ministry of Christ, the Twelve are introduced to Satan's counterfeit Christ, the man who will seek to destroy the elect of God in the last days. There can be no doubt that the "Abomination of Desolation" is Antichrist, the "beast" of Revelation 12–13, who will have "a mouth speaking arrogant words and blasphemies and authority to act for forty-two months" (Rev. 13:5), the one Paul refers to as the "man of lawlessness," who "takes his seat in the temple of God, displaying himself as being God" (2 Thess. 2:3–4).

Going back to Daniel 9:27, the passage to which Christ had just referred, where the "one who makes desolate" (Antichrist) is first introduced, we see this time of persecution associated with the *midpoint* of the seven-year tribulation period.

At the beginning of this final, seven-year tribulation period, Antichrist

> "will make a firm covenant with the many for one week, *but in the middle of the week* he [Antichrist] will put a stop to sacrifice and grain offering; *and on the wing of abominations will come one who makes desolate* [referring again to Antichrist]" (Dan. 9:27, emphasis added).[5]

It will be at the "middle of the week," at the midpoint of the seven-year tribulation period, that Antichrist will be revealed as the "one who makes desolate." Christ then warns those of *you* (Matt. 24:15) living in Jerusalem in the last days, explaining what *you* must do, immediately, if *you* see the Abomination of Desolation (Antichrist) standing in the holy place of the temple:

> (16) "Let those who are in Judea flee to the mountains; (17) let him who is on the housetop not go down to get the things out that are in his house; (18) and let him who is in the field not turn back to get his cloak. (19) But woe to those who are with child and to those who nurse babes in those days! (20) But pray that *your* flight may not be in the winter, or on a Sabbath; (21) for then there will be a great tribulation [persecution], such as has not occurred since the beginning of the world until now, nor ever shall. (22) And unless those days had been cut short, no life would have been saved; *but for the sake of the elect those days shall be cut short*" (**MATT. 24:16–22**, emphasis added).

As this passage clearly states in verse 21, the atrocities of Antichrist against those who stand firm for Christ (or stand

---

5. The Hebrew word translated "week" in Dan. 9:27 refers to a "unit of seven" of anything. It is commonly and rightly understood that a week in this and similar contexts is a Hebraism used to refer to a unit of seven years (see Dan. 12:7, 11–12). Comparing that usage with Rev. 12:6 and 13:5, one must conclude that Daniel's week refers to individual units of seven years each.

firm against Antichrist, as some Jews will do, according to
Dan. 12:1; cf. Rev. 12:13–17) will be the worst persecution the
true children of God (*you*—the elect) have ever known since
the beginning of time. This is when "they will deliver *you* to
tribulation, and will kill *you*, and *you* will be hated by all nations on account of My name" (Matt. 24:9, emphasis added).

Can you begin to understand why Christ warned His disciples not to be misled (Matt. 24:4) and to listen carefully to what
He was teaching them?

Yet those who hold to the pretribulation Rapture position
insist that "the elect" who will undergo this horrible time of
persecution will not be the church, but the nation of Israel.
However, as we saw in the last chapter (the first point dealing
with the wrath of God), Israel is not saved until after the seven-
year tribulation period is complete. Referring to this time of
Gentile domination of Jerusalem, Christ had earlier, while still
in the temple, taught His disciples that "Jerusalem will be
trampled under foot by the Gentiles until the times of the Gentiles be fulfilled" (Luke 21:24). Paul specifically tells the
church in Rome that Israel will not be saved "until the fulness
of the Gentiles has come in" (Rom. 11:25–26), paralleling
Daniel's prophecy that "everlasting righteousness" will be
brought in to the nation of Israel only after the seven-year tribulation period (seventieth week) is complete (Dan. 9:24).
Thus, the elect of God—*you*—who for the sake of Christ's
name will undergo persecution at the hands of Antichrist at
the midpoint of the tribulation period (Matt. 24:9) cannot be
the newly saved nation of Israel because she will not be saved
until after the tribulation period is complete, until after "the
fulness of the Gentiles has come in"! This is why the prophet
Amos, when referring to Israel's persecution in the last days,
explains that ". . . you [of Israel] who are longing for the Day
of the LORD, for what purpose will the Day of the LORD be to
you? It will be darkness and not light; as when a man flees

from a lion [the persecution] and a bear [the Day of the Lord] meets him . . ." (Amos 5:18–19a).

In other words, unsaved Israel will not be rescued—as God's elect will be—before the Day of the Lord begins. To unsaved Israel, the Day of the Lord will be a day of darkness, not light.

In addition, the very words used by the writers argue that the "elect" undergoing Antichrist's persecution, is a reference to the true bond-servants of Christ within the church in general. Judge for yourselves. The word translated "elect" (*eklektós*) in verse 22, although used several times in the New Testament to refer to Christ and to special angels (as opposed to fallen angels), is most commonly used to refer to genuine Christians—individually or as a community—chosen before the foundation of the world. If in every other instance in which *eklektós* is used (outside the exemptions just mentioned) the word refers to the true bond-servants of Christ, why should the use of this word in the Olivet Discourse of Christ be understood any differently?

In a parallel passage recorded in the book of Revelation, referring to the same time of intense tribulation, those persecuted by Antichrist are called "the saints" rather than "the elect."

> And it was given to him [Antichrist] to make war with the saints and to overcome them (Rev. 13:7a).

John is referring to a group of men and women, "who keep the commandments of God and hold to the testimony of Jesus," whom Satan attempts to destroy after God has thwarted his efforts to destroy "the woman"—Israel (Rev. 12:13–17). Obviously from the context, "the elect" and "the saints" are one and the same and are clearly someone other than Israel, whom John refers to simply as "the woman."

Thus, by comparing Scripture with Scripture, we see that the Olivet Discourse refers to those persecuted as *the elect of God,* whereas the book of Revelation refers to them simply as *the saints.* And, as with "elect," the underlying Greek word (*hágios,* translated "saints" or "holy") can, like the word *eklektós,* refer to Christ or His angels or, when referring to human beings, to the genuine bond-servants of Christ within the church.

A possible explanation of why the term "church" is not used in these two critical passages is that when the church is faced with the tribulation associated with Antichrist (Matt. 24:9; cf. vv. 21–22), it will not be the church in general that "endures to the end" (vv. 10–13); instead, it will be the genuine bond-servants of Christ (His elect or saints) who will prefer to endure the wrath of Satan rather than the wrath of God (v. 9). This is why Christ refers to them as *you.* The rest of the professing church will escape this terrible time of persecution because they will "fall away" (v. 10) and their love for Christ "will grow cold" (v. 12) as they choose to worship Antichrist rather then die for the sake of the true Christ. *It will be the church in general that will fall away into apostasy in the last days. It is the elect of God (the saints) who will endure Antichrist's persecution. That is precisely why terms such as "the elect" and "the saints" are used instead of the word* church *to describe the faithful who will choose death over compromise!* (More is said to this issue in chapter 7.)

The other important point in this passage is the promise God gives His elect: to *cut short* (from the Greek verb *kolobóō*) the days of their persecution by Antichrist.[6]

6. *Koloboó* basically means "to maim or amputate" and is used here in the passive voice, indicating that the action happens *to* the subject, in this case the days of great tribulation. This word does not mean "to limit" something; it means to cut something short. *In this sentence, the subject to which this verb is connected, is Antichrist's persecution, not the man or his forty-two-month authority to rule.*

Now let us continue with the text of Jesus' warning. Because we know that the Abomination of Desolation will show his true colors when he desecrates the temple in Jerusalem, Antichrist's persecution will begin in Jerusalem. For that reason Jesus begins by warning those living in Jerusalem: if you should see these things begin to happen, you should drop everything and flee (vv. 16–20). Some will make it to safety, but even those who succeed in finding a place to hide will not escape potential trouble. So, to those who do manage to escape, He gives a separate warning:

> (23) "Then [to those of you who have safely fled into hiding], if anyone says to *you*, 'Behold, here is the Christ,' or 'There He is,' do not believe him. (24) For false Christs and false prophets will arise and will show great signs and wonders, so as to mislead, if possible, even *the elect.* (25) Behold, I have told *you* in advance. (26) If therefore they say *to you*, 'Behold, He is in the wilderness,' do not go forth, or, 'Behold, He is in the inner rooms,' do not believe them" (**MATT. 24:23–26**, emphasis added).

Those (of you) in hiding must not let yourselves be lured out by false Christs, prophets, or promises! The false Christs and false prophets will be extremely persuasive, showing great signs and wonders capable of misleading even the elect, *if possible.* Thank God for the phrase "if possible." Personally I don't think it will be possible to mislead the elect if the elect heed this warning of Christ. But even the possibility is frightening. All the more reason for Christ to begin His discourse with the warning: "See to it that no one misleads you" (24:4).

But then, in the midst of all the bad news, Christ gives His disciples the *good* news: some of God's elect will escape the clutches of Antichrist and his false prophets!

In perhaps the most important verses of the Olivet Discourse for God's elect who faithfully endure to the end, Christ now answers His disciples' question concerning the sign of His coming and of the end of the age.

(22) "For the sake of the elect those days [of great persecution or tribulation] shall be cut short. . . . (27) For just as the lightning comes from the east, and flashes even to the west, so shall the coming of the Son of Man be. . . . (29) immediately after the tribulation of those days the sun will be darkened, and the moon will not give its light, and the stars will fall from the sky, and the powers of the heavens will be shaken, (30) and then the sign of the Son of Man will appear in the sky, and then all the tribes of the earth will mourn, and they will see the Son of Man coming on the clouds of the sky with power and great glory. (31) And He will send forth His angels with a great trumpet and they will gather together His elect from the four winds, from one end of the sky to the other" (MATT. 24:22, 27, 29–31).

The good news is that Antichrist's persecution will not go on endlessly, but will be cut short by the event that will occur when the sign of the Day of the Lord is given in the heavens, announcing that the day of God's wrath has come, when the angels of Christ "gather together His elect from the four winds, from one end of the sky to the other." Abruptly remove the objects of Antichrist's persecution and, by definition, his persecution against them must come to an abrupt end.

Keeping this abrupt ending in mind—when the persecution of God's elect is cut short—we will now look at the three separate events that will occur, one right after the other, that will bring Antichrist's persecution of God's elect to its abrupt ending: (1) the sign of the end of the age; (2) the sign of Christ's coming coupled with the actual coming of Christ; and (3) the gathering together of God's elect from the four winds.

The Sign of the End of the Age

As we saw in the previous chapter (the second point dealing with the sign of the Day of the Lord), God, through His prophet Joel, has promised to give a sign in the sun, moon, and stars "before the great and awesome day of the LORD comes" (Joel

2:31b). Now, here in the Olivet Discourse, Christ specifically refers to this sign as "the sign of the end of the age."

Later, Christ would instruct the writer of the book of Revelation that when this sign in the sun, moon, and stars is given in the heavens, it will be accompanied by a great earthquake:

> (12) And there was a great earthquake; and the sun became black as sackcloth made of hair, and the whole moon became like blood; (13) and the stars of the sky fell to the earth, as a fig tree casts its unripe figs when shaken by a great wind. (14) And the sky was split apart like a scroll when it is rolled up; and every mountain and island were moved out of their places (Rev. 6:12–14).

Putting our key text from Matthew 24 together with these passages from Joel and Revelation 6, we see that when the sign is given in the sun, moon, and stars *before* the great and awesome Day of the Lord begins, the natural lights in the heavens will be extinguished. Thus, the sign of the Day of the Lord will, in effect, turn the universe into a black hole into which the sign of Christ's coming will now be given. This, then, brings us to the second event.

The Sign of Christ's Coming

Our key Olivet Discourse passage tells us that the sign of Christ's coming will be like lightning coming from the east and flashing to the west (Matt. 24:27). Thus, the sign of His coming will be the visual manifestation of God's glory *returning* to earth (as predicted by the prophet Ezekiel [Ezek. 43:1–2a]). When the sign of Christ's coming is seen coming from the east and going to the west—like lightning—the glory of Christ will burst into the blackened atmosphere brought about by the sign of the end of the age, and then the world "will see the Son of Man coming on the clouds of the sky with power and great glory"!

Isaiah, speaking of this glorious return of Christ, refers to "the splendor of His majesty, when He arises to make the earth tremble" (Isa. 2:19b). Titus, too, referring to the blessed hope of every true believer, says that we should be looking for "the appearing of the *glory* of our great God and Savior, Christ Jesus" (Titus 2:13b, emphasis added). Mere words cannot begin to describe the wonder of it all. And then, the all-important third event will occur.

The Gathering of God's Elect

Then, when Christ appears, "He will send forth His angels with a great trumpet and they will gather together His elect from the four winds, from one end of the sky to the other" (Matt. 24:31). There is your rapture of the faithful who endure to the end! Plain and simple.

But notice the timing of *when* the elect of God are gathered together, from one end of the sky to the other: not until *after* the Abomination of Desolation is seen standing in the holy place, *after* the great persecution by Antichrist has been initiated against the saints of God, *after* many professing Christians fall away and lose their love for Christ, *after* two back-to-back signs have been displayed in the heavens, and *after* the entire world sees the Son of Man coming on the clouds of the sky, with power and great glory—*but*, as the writers of the New Testament had often promised the church, *before* the wrath of God is poured out upon the wicked that remain. It will be these events, tied together, that will bring Antichrist's persecution of God's elect to an abrupt ending. For the true bond-servants of Christ, deliverance. For the unsaved nation of Israel, escape from the "lion," only to face the "bear" when the Day of the Lord begins.

Remember, earlier in the Olivet Discourse Christ explained it this way:

(9) "Then they will deliver you to tribulation [persecution], and will kill you, and you will be hated by all nations on account of My name. . . . (13) But the one who endures [the tribulation] to the end, he shall be saved [delivered]. (14) And this gospel of the kingdom shall be preached in the whole world for a witness to all the nations, and then the end [God's wrath] shall come" (Matt. 24:9, 13–14).

The true bond-servants of Christ who endure the persecution of Antichrist (v. 9) to the end of the age (v. 13a) will be delivered (v. 13b); they will be raptured out of the midst of the persecution they have been undergoing (v. 9), and then the end shall come (v. 14).

The End of the Age

"The end," "the end of the age," "the Day of the Lord," and "the day of judgment" are different terms that all refer to the same thing: the time when God's wrath will be poured out upon the wicked world that remains after the genuine children of God have been "rescued," "delivered," "saved," or "raptured" from Antichrist's persecution.

Christ now makes reference to this time of God's wrath by using the same illustration He had used previously. Earlier, as we discussed in some detail in the last point in chapter 3, He had explained to the disciples that these two events, the Rapture and God's wrath, would occur on the same day, using the illustration of Noah and the Flood to make His point (Luke 17:26–27). Now, once again, He tells them that

(37) "The coming of the Son of Man will be just like the days of Noah. (38) For as in those days which were before the flood *they* were eating and drinking, *they* were marrying and giving in marriage, until the day that Noah entered the ark, (39) and *they* did not understand until the flood came and took *them* all away; so

shall the coming of the Son of Man be. (40) . . . one will be taken, and one will be left" (**MATT. 24:37–40**, emphasis added).

Notice it is *they*, not *you* who are caught unawares at the coming of the Son of Man. Two verses later, Christ exhorts *you* to "be on the alert, for *you* do not know which day *your* Lord is coming" (v. 42, emphasis added). At least a quarter of a century later, Peter uses the identical comparison in making his case concerning the severity of the Day of the Lord that occurs in connection with "His [Christ's] coming":

(3) Know this first of all, that *in the last days mockers* will come with their mocking, following after *their* own lusts, (4) and saying, *"Where is the promise of His coming?"* . . . (5) For when *they* maintain this, it escapes their notice that by the word of God the heavens existed long ago and the earth was formed out of water and by water, (6) through which *the world at that time was destroyed, being flooded with water.* (7) But the present heavens and earth by His word are being reserved for fire, kept for the *day of judgment and destruction of ungodly men.* . . . (10) [For] *the day of the Lord* will come like a thief, in which the heavens will pass away with a roar and the elements will be destroyed with intense heat, and the earth and its works will be burned up (2 Pet. 3:3–7, 10, emphasis added).

And again, as Christ did to His disciples, Peter exhorts the true believer that "since all these things are to be destroyed in this way, what sort of people ought *you* to be, in holy conduct and godliness, looking for and hastening the coming of the day of God . . ." (vv. 11–12a, emphasis added). After one understands the devastation associated with the Day of the Lord, is it any wonder that God promises His elect that they will never undergo His wrath?

Thus, the Olivet Discourse not only refers to the wrath of Satan through his minion Antichrist ("the Abomination of Desolation . . . when [he] will kill you"), but to the deliverance of the faithful from Satan's wrath ("He will send forth His angels with a great trumpet and they will gather together His elect from the four winds") as well as a reference to the wrath of God that follows during the Day of the Lord ("the flood came and took them all away; so shall the coming of the Son of Man be").

Summing It Up

The Olivet Discourse recorded in Matthew 24 is an overview of end time events and, as such, is clear concerning the sequence of events that will occur before the return of Christ for His own (His elect, His saints) and the commencement of the end of the age. This sequence should be understood and remembered as we continue our study concerning the timing of the Rapture.

In this general overview, Christ gave His disciples the following sequence of events:

> *First,* the warning: "See to it that no one misleads you" (v. 4).
> *Then,* "many will come in My name, saying 'I am the Christ'" (v. 5).
> *Then,* there will be "wars and rumors of wars," *but that is not yet the end of the age* (v. 6).
> *Then,* there will be "famines and earthquakes," but all these things are merely the beginning of birth pangs (vv. 7–8).
> *Then,* the Abomination of Desolation will be seen "standing in the holy place" (v. 15).
> *Then,* there will be "great tribulation" (vv. 9, 21).
> *Then,* they will "kill you, and you will be hated by all nations on account of My name" (v. 9).
> *Then,* "many will fall away . . . most people's love will grow cold" (vv. 10–12).
> *Then,* "the one who endures to the end . . . shall be saved [delivered]" (v. 13),
> *but not before* the "gospel of the kingdom shall be preached in the whole world for a witness to all the nations" (v. 14).

OLIVET DISCOURSE — Matthew 24

Combined Sequence of Events

24:4	**WARNING** To God's Elect
24:5	**FALSE CHRISTS**
24:6	**WARS**
24:7	**FAMINES**
24:9, 21 24:21	**THE GREAT TRIBULATION** Against God's Elect
24:9, 22	Death
24:10, 24	Apostasy
24:29	**SIGN OF THE END OF THE AGE** Sun, Moon and Stars
24:30, 27	**SIGN OF CHRIST'S COMING** Like Lightning
24:30	**THE COMING OF CHRIST**
24:13, 31	**THE DELIVERANCE OF CHRIST'S ELECT** The Rapture
24:14, 37-39	**THE WRATH OF GOD** The End of the Age or The Day of the Lord

"Then the end shall come" (v. 14), the day of God's great wrath.

After this general overview, Christ gives specific information concerning the sequence of events that will "cut short" the days of Antichrist's great persecution against the elect of God (vv. 22, 29):

First, "the sun will be darkened, and the moon will not give its light, and the stars will fall from the sky" (v. 29).

Then, "the sign of the Son of Man will appear in the sky" (v. 30), "as the lightning comes from the east, and flashes even to the west" (v. 27).

Then, you will "see the Son of Man coming on the clouds of the sky with power and great glory" (v. 30).

Then, Christ's angels will "gather together His elect from the four winds, from one end of the sky to the other" (v. 31; cf. v. 13), thus removing the target of Antichrist's Satanic-inspired wrath—the elect of God—abruptly ending his persecution of them.

And then, finally, the day of the God's wrath—the end of the age—will come (vv. 14, 37–39).

But When?

The sequence Christ gives to His disciples in the Olivet Discourse is critical to our knowing when the Rapture will occur in relationship to the persecution by Antichrist. But He does not tell us when in relationship to time. Christ says a few verses later:

> "But of that day and hour no one knows, not even the angels of heaven, nor the Son, but the Father alone" (**MATT. 24:36**).

Even after the events described in the Olivet Discourse actually begin to occur, no one—including the angels in heaven or even Christ in His humanity—knows the exact "day and hour" when Christ will return to rescue His saints from Antichrist's persecution. Yet Paul says, "You, brethren, are not in darkness, that the day [of the Lord] should overtake you like a thief" (1 Thess. 5:4).

The Olivet Discourse teaches us that the return of Christ will occur sometime during the second half of the final seven-year period, *after* Antichrist has begun his persecution of the elect, the saints of God, *but before* his forty-two months of allotted time of authority is finished, while the rest of the world is going on, as usual, eating, drinking, marrying, "as in the days of Noah." That is why the return of Christ will come upon those living in darkness "just like a thief in the night . . . but *you, brethren,* are not in darkness, that the day should overtake you like a thief" (1 Thess. 5:2, 4, emphasis added). The return of Christ will become imminent, at "any moment," only after Antichrist takes his seat in the temple and demands the worship of the world at the midpoint of the seven-year tribulation period.

Although we cannot know the day or the hour, Christ did tell His disciples that we should learn from the parable of the fig tree:

> (32) "When its branch has already become tender, and puts forth its leaves, you know that summer is near; (33) even so you too, when you see all these things, recognize that He is near, right at the door. (34) Truly I say to you, this generation will not pass away until all these things take place" (MATT. 24:32–34).

If you take this illustration at face value, its meaning is self-explanatory. When the branches of fig trees became tender and put forth their leaves, everyone living in Israel knew that summer was near. Likewise, the generation that sees the events described in the Olivet Discourse begin to transpire should know that the coming of Christ is near.

The fulfillment of many biblical prophecies (like Dan. 9:24–27) has extended over long periods of time. But this prophecy concerning Christ's coming and the end of the age

will be started and fulfilled within the lifetime of the generation that sees these things begin. Why? Because the Lord instructed Daniel that from beginning to end, it will be less than
a seven-year period in total: from Israel's covenant with Antichrist, to the beginning birth pangs, to the hard labor associated with the persecution of God's elect, to the coming of
Christ to rescue His elect and begin the destruction of the
wicked who remain at the end of the age.

In 1948, Israel became a nation. In 1967, Israel regained
control of Jerusalem. These two events are critical; they had to
occur before the events outlined in the Olivet Discourse could
commence. Summer is not yet come, but the branch—God's
ancient people, the Jews, so to speak—is definitely tender and
the leaves are beginning to bud. Therefore, "let us not sleep as
others do, but let us be alert and sober" (1 Thess. 5:6), watch-
ing what is happening in the Middle East as never before.

Is Matthew Applicable?

Christ's teaching in the Olivet Discourse concerning the signs of His coming and the end of the age (the Day of the Lord) are straightforward. The Olivet Discourse is precise as to when the signs will be given in the heavens. The persecution associated with Antichrist will be cut short by the events that occur in association with the sign given in the sun, moon, and stars, when the Son of Man will be seen coming with power and great glory, sending His angels forth to gather together the elect of God from one end of the sky to the other. The sequence of these end time events has never been the question or the issue. But those holding to the pretribulation view have made the context in which these events occur another matter altogether and, for that reason, a matter of serious debate. The implications of which context you choose have overwhelming significance and possible consequences for the church in general. Therefore, before we look at the specific teaching of Paul concerning when the Rapture will occur (in the next chapter), we will first look carefully at the context of this controversial discourse to Christ's disciples as recorded in the book of Matthew.

Those holding to the pretribulation view, although willing to admit that certain of "the elect of God" will go through the great tribulation (see Matt. 24:21–22, 24, 31), try to keep the church out of this time of persecution by refusing to recognize that the Olivet Discourse has anything to do with the Rapture or that "the elect of God" has anything whatsoever to do with the church. Instead, as we saw in the previous chapter, they maintain that this passage is primarily instruction for Jews who are converted to Christ after the Rapture takes place. Thus, the elect of God who undergo the persecution of Antichrist will not be the church per se, but those Jewish men and women who come to Christ after the Rapture of God's church-age saints. The Olivet Discourse, they say, was given to Christ's disciples in view of their Jewish lineage, not in view of the fact that they were soon to become the founding fathers of the church. The Olivet Discourse, therefore, is in reference to Christ's coming to fight the battle of Armageddon, an event that they see happening *at the very end* of the seven-year tribulation period, at least seven years after the Rapture has taken place (in part, using the Flood account discussed in the last point of chapter 2 to help make their point).

The Parousia Problem

But taking the position described just above has serious logical and biblical problems associated with it, to say nothing of the problems they have when referring to the Flood account to make their argument. If the coming (the Greek word *parousía*) of Christ referred to in the Olivet Discourse is indeed a reference to the battle of Armageddon, an event that occurs *at the end* of the tribulation period, then, by definition, it must be different than the coming (*parousía*) of Christ associated with the Rapture (1 Thess. 4:15), which they teach will occur *before* this final seven-year period begins. In other words, the church should then be looking for the second coming *(parousía)* of Christ but Israel should be waiting for His third coming *(parousía)*!

At this point, allow me to give a brief description of the Greek word *parousía*. This is a noun, which carries the sense of arrival or active presence, and should not be interpreted as if it were a verb. *Parousía*, as an active presence, has a powerful meaning that can be lost in its translation into English. In Christ's time the word was often used to refer to the arrival of a king or a general, and the picture painted by the *parousía* of Christ in the Olivet Discourse is poignant. The citizens of God's Kingdom, the Kingdom of Heaven, embattled by Satan through the hand of Antichrist, anxiously await the coming *(parousía)* or arrival of their King, when He will rescue His subjects and destroy the enemy.

Therefore, the Greek noun *parousía* refers to Christ's coming as an event, not as an activity. It is not a verb, referring to His movement from one place to another. If a verbal meaning were intended, a Greek verb like *érchomai* would have been used instead. When the disciples asked about the sign of His "coming," they used the noun, *parousía*, not the verb, *érchomai*.

The classic, uncontested Rapture passage is found in 1 Thessalonians 4:13–17. Although we will delve into this passage in greater detail in the next chapter, I want to point out the language Paul uses in connection with the coming of Christ for the Rapture of His saints.

(15) For this we say to you by the word of the Lord, that we who are alive, and remain until the *coming [parousía] of the Lord,* shall not precede those who have fallen asleep. (16) For the Lord Himself will descend from heaven with a shout, and with the voice of the archangel, and with the trumpet of God; and the dead in Christ shall rise first. (17) Then we who are alive and remain *shall be caught up together with them in the clouds to meet the Lord in the*

air, and thus we shall always be with the Lord (1 Thess. 4:15–17, emphasis added).

Notice that the Rapture—"caught up together with them in the clouds to meet the Lord in the air" (v. 17)—is associated directly with the *coming* of Christ (v. 15) which, using the English translation alone, could be understood as either a noun or a verb. But the Greek word Paul uses here is *parousía,* the noun, the same Greek word the disciples used when they asked Christ what the sign of His coming (*parousía*) would be.

In Paul's second letter to the believers at Thessalonica, the Rapture is again referred to, directly and indisputably.

> Now we request you, brethren, with regard to the *coming [parousía] of our Lord Jesus Christ, and our gathering together to Him,* that . . . (2 Thess. 2:1, emphasis added).

As in his first letter to the Thessalonians, Paul once again uses the Greek noun *parousía* when referring to the coming of Christ, that is, for the purposes of gathering together His saints to Him at the Rapture.

Comparing Scripture with Scripture, it becomes apparent that John likewise admonishes the church, not Israel, to look for the *parousía*—the event, not the activity—of Christ, and it becomes clear from the context that he, too, is referring to the Rapture, not to the battle of Armageddon. In his first epistle, addressed to Christians all over Asia Minor, the apostle says,

> And now, little children, abide in Him [Christ], so that when He appears, we may have confidence and not shrink away from Him in shame at His coming [*parousía*] (1 John 2:28).

Now this is where the problems begin if one tries to make the *parousía* of Christ in the Olivet Discourse a reference to the battle of Armageddon. Unlike the passages we have just looked at, which clearly connect the *parousía* of Christ with the Rapture, *there is not one passage in the entire Bible that directly connects the* parousía *of Christ with the battle of Armageddon.*

Having looked at the classic Rapture passage recorded in 1 Thessalonians 4, we must in fairness also look at the Armageddon passage recorded in the book of Revelation—the only passage in the New Testament that deals specifically and unequivocally with the battle of Armageddon:

> (11) And I saw heaven opened; and behold, a white horse, and He who sat upon it is called Faithful and True; and in righteousness He judges and wages war. . . . (14) And the armies which are in heaven, clothed in fine linen, white and clean, were following Him on white horses. (15) And from His mouth comes a sharp sword, so that with it He may smite the nations. . . . (19) And I saw the beast and the kings of the earth and their armies, assembled to make war against Him who sat upon the horse, and against His army. (20) And the beast was seized, and . . . thrown alive into the lake of fire . . . (Rev. 19:11, 14–15, 19–20).

Unlike the Rapture passage, not once in this entire account of the battle of Armageddon is the *parousía* of Christ ever referred to. In fact, the language doesn't even hint at it.

In spite of that fact, however, if the parousía *of Christ referred to in the Olivet Discourse were indeed in reference to the battle of Armageddon, then, as I said earlier, there must be two separate returns of Christ, a second and a third* parousía *of Christ as it were, the second occurring sometime before the seven-year tribulation period (where those holding to the pretribulation Rapture view place it) and the third occurring at the very end of it (where the battle of Armageddon is fought).*

However, those who accept the Olivet Discourse in its most natural, normal, customary sense, see only a single *parousía* of Christ that would include different activities occurring after the rapture of His saints (i.e., the wrath of God upon the wicked world remaining, the salvation of Israel, the final battle of Armageddon, etc.), as was the case with His first coming (i.e., His birth, His baptism, His crucifixion, and His resurrection).

The Day of the Lord Problem

Subscribing to this view causes an even greater problem than the mere fact that this position necessitates a second and third *parousía* of Christ. *This position would also necessitate having two separate and distinct Days of the Lord, each of which, by definition, would have God destroying all the wicked living upon earth at that time (Zeph. 1:18; cf. 2 Pet. 3:7).*

The Olivet Discourse clearly teaches that the wrath of God (i.e., the end of the age that will be announced with signs in the sun, moon, and stars) will immediately follow this specific *parousía* of Christ ("and then the end shall come . . . as in the days of Noah"). The pretribulationists teach that this is in reference to the battle of Armageddon. Paul, in the classic Rapture passage, likewise instructs the Thessalonian church that the Rapture will occur when the Day of the Lord begins (see 1 Thess. 4:15–5:2). Thus, the context of this Day of the Lord is the *parousía* of Christ at the Rapture.

If indeed the *parousía* of Christ is referring to two completely different comings of Christ—as those holding to the pretribulation position insist—one before the tribulation period and one at the end of it, separated by at least seven years, then both events must be accompanied by separate Days of the Lord. Just look with me, for a moment, at the total destruction associated with that Day of the Lord that occurs at the second coming of Christ, when the true church is raptured, supposedly seven years *prior* to the final and last day of God's wrath associated with His third coming at the battle of Armageddon!

In this classic Day of the Lord passage, Peter instructs the scattered Gentile believers that

(3) . . . in the last days mockers will come with their mocking, following after their own lusts, (4) and saying, "Where is the promise of His coming [*parousía*]? . . . (7) But the present heavens and earth by His word are being reserved for fire, kept for the day of judgment and destruction of ungodly men. (10) . . . in which the heavens will pass away with a roar and the elements will be destroyed with intense heat, and the earth and its works will be burned up. (11) Since all these things are to be destroyed in this way, what sort of people ought you to be in holy conduct and godliness, (12) looking for and hastening the coming of the day of God, on account of which the heavens will be destroyed by burning, and the elements will melt with intense heat! (2 Pet. 3:3–4, 7, 10–12).

If there are two separate Days of the Lord that will occur in the last days, one that occurs at the Rapture as described by Paul in 1 Thessalonians 4–5 (before the tribulation period) and the second when Christ comes at the battle of Armageddon as described in the Olivet Discourse (at the end of the tribulation period), then clearly the passage in Peter has to be referring to the Day of the Lord that occurs at the Rapture, before the tribulation period begins! Why? Because this is instruction written to Gentiles— remember, those holding to the pretribulation Rapture position make the instruction contained in the Olivet Discourse primarily applicable to the Jews because the church has been raptured at least seven years earlier. Second, the Day of the Lord described in Peter speaks of the "*present* heavens and earth [being] reserved for fire, kept for the day of judgment and destruction of ungodly men," the idea being that this passage is referring to the next cataclysm the earth will undergo after the Flood of Noah. By their own definition, then, this passage in 2 Peter must refer to the *parousía* of Christ associated with the rapture of the church, which comes seven years before the *parousía* associated with the battle of Armageddon! And lastly, the Gentile believers to whom Peter wrote are told to look for and hasten the coming of this specific Day of God (v. 12). If they have been raptured seven years earlier, however, that will be a hard instruction to follow!

Equally important, I hope you have noticed the totality of God's wrath: "the heavens will pass away with a roar and the elements will be destroyed with intense heat, and the earth and its works will be burned up" (v. 10).

Now, think about that for a moment and use a little common sense. If God wipes out the entire wicked human race that remains after His saints have been removed at the Rapture (as our passage here clearly indicates), and this event occurs approximately seven years *before* the battle of Armageddon is fought, who, then, would be left for God to fight seven years later? And how will Antichrist build a worldwide empire at the midpoint of the tribulation period, if the people who are the children of Satan (1 John 3:10) have all been killed just three-and-a-half years earlier? And even if the destruction described in 2 Peter 3 could possibly leave a few survivors, what's left on earth to rule over, anyway? Do you begin to see the problems associated with a position that has no biblical support?

But the truth of the matter is this: there is absolutely no evidence of two separate and distinct Days of the Lord even hinted at in Scripture, any more than there is any biblical evidence of more than one *parousía* of Christ in the last days. In both Old and New Testaments, only one Day of the Lord is ever referred to in connection with the last days, when the citizens of the Kingdom of Satan will be destroyed by God's wrath and the Kingdom of Christ will be established upon earth. The very definition of what God will accomplish in His day makes more than one time of wrath unnecessary, if not impossible.

The prewrath view sees only one *parousía* of Christ and one Day of the Lord, both occurring when Christ comes to rapture the faithful and then begins His systematic destruction of the wicked who remain (the Day of the Lord)!

Surely if there were to be more than one *parousía* in the last days, or more than one time of total destruction of God's enemies, such a distinction would be clear in Scripture in order to avoid confusion on this extremely important matter. But just the opposite is true. Throughout both the Old and New Testaments—and even in intertestamental Jewish literature (the Pseudepigrapha and the Apocrypha)—only two advents of Christ are ever mentioned: the first to die and be raised, and the second to rescue and judge. As would be expected, therefore, the Greek word *parousía* is always in the singular, never the plural, as is the concept of a single, final time of God's fiery wrath (likened to the *single time* God destroyed the earth by water in the days of Noah).

Other Related Problems

But there are additional problems that must be resolved if one attempts to make the Olivet Discourse recorded in Matthew applicable only to Israel. If indeed this is true, then how do we interpret this same Olivet Discourse as recorded in the gospel of Mark, or the parallel instruction Christ gives His disciples in the temple (what I like to refer to as the Temple Prelude to the Olivet Discourse) as recorded in Luke 21? No one can seriously or effectively argue that Mark's primary audience was Jewish, and it is generally accepted that Luke's gospel, specifically dedicated to Theophilus, was directed to *all* Gentiles.

It is also more than a little interesting that Matthew—written primarily to Jews—*is the only gospel* that even refers specifically to the church! In chapter 16, Christ says to Peter, "'You are Peter, and upon this rock I will build My *church*; and the gates of Hades shall not overpower it'" (v. 18). In this passage, Christ obviously was referring to Himself as the foundation of the church, instruction He felt was important for His disciples to know in that they were soon to become the founding fathers of the church. Later, in chapter 18, referring to church discipline, the Lord says, "And if he [an unrepentant believer] refuses to listen to them, tell it to the *church*; and if he refuses to listen even to the *church*, let him be to you as a Gentile and a tax-gatherer" (v. 17).

Still later, in 26:17–30, Christ gives His disciples instruction concerning observance of the Lord's Supper—which could not possibly have relevance to anyone other than true believers within the church in general. This specific instruction pertaining to the crucifixion of Christ has untold significance for the church, but none at all for the unsaved nation of Israel. How is it then that one decides to throw out the Olivet Discourse, making it applicable only to Israel, when everything taught in the larger context of this discourse pertains directly to the church?

The Great Commission Problem

But the greatest hurdle one must cross is found in the last two verses of the final chapter of that gospel, often referred to as the Great Commission.

> (19) "Go therefore and make disciples of all the nations, baptizing them in the name of the Father and the Son and the Holy Spirit, (20) teaching them to observe all that I commanded you; and lo, I am with you always, even to the end of the age" (Matt. 28:19–20).

Few evangelical Christians would deny the importance of that instruction to the church. Since first uttered by our Lord, it has been the church's marching orders, commissioning us to send missionaries around the world, to make disciples of all nations, and to instruct them in the things of the Lord.

But look carefully at the text of the Great Commission itself. There we see that Christ's disciples were told to teach the new converts from all the nations "to observe *all that I [Christ] commanded you*" (v. 20). What does "all that I commanded you" mean if it does not include everything Christ taught His disciples in that particular gospel, the gospel of Matthew? The commands of Christ to His disciples must, in fact, include *all* of His teachings given to His disciples in *all four gospels*. They are the only firsthand record we have of His teaching. We certainly dare not limit "all that I commanded you" to Christ's teachings found *only* in the other gospels or in selected parts of Matthew. And even if we try to limit that command to the three other gospels, how do we exclude the Olivet Discourse recorded in Mark and the Temple Prelude recorded in Luke? Which commands of Christ, in which of the gospels, are we to teach the new disciples? Who decides which commands should be taught and which ones should not? The only limitation Christ gives His disciples is that they teach these new converts *all* that He had instructed *them*. Using the limitation given us by Christ (rather than the limitation imposed on us by pretribulationists intent upon protecting a premise devoid of biblical support), then, our decision on what is applicable to the church and what isn't becomes easy to discern!

In Matthew 23, Christ had warned, "'Woe to you, *scribes and Pharisees*, hypocrites, because you shut off the kingdom of heaven from men; for you do not enter in yourselves, nor do you allow those who are entering to go in. Woe. . . . Woe. . . . Woe. . . . Woe . . .'" (see 23:13–39). Whom was Christ instructing in this passage? His disciples? No, this instruction was explicitly to the scribes and the Pharisees. Therefore, this *was not* instruction that had to be passed on to new generations of believers.

On the other hand, the Olivet Discourse was instruction to His disciples. It begins with "See to it that no one misleads *you*" and goes on to use the personal pronoun *you* at least ten times in the heart of His instruction concerning the timing of His *parousía* (Matt. 24:4–31). And so, by the very words of

Christ at the end of the book of Matthew, this instruction *was* to be taught to new believers in fulfillment of the Great Commission.

Comparing Scripture with Scripture, we find that Paul warned Timothy:

> (3) If anyone advocates a different doctrine, and does not agree *with sound words, those of our Lord Jesus Christ,* and with the doctrine conforming to godliness, (4) he is conceited and understands nothing; but *he has a morbid interest in controversial questions and disputes about words, out of which arise envy, strife, abusive language, evil suspicions, (5) and constant friction between men of depraved mind and deprived of the truth* . . . (1 Tim. 6:3–5, emphasis added).

Paul is unambiguously clear: the "sound words" that are to be taught to the churches are "those of our Lord Jesus Christ"! He did not say "some" of the words of Christ or "only" the words of Christ found in certain places or certain gospels. Nor did he distinguish which specific words were to be considered the "sound words . . . of our Lord Jesus Christ" and which words of Christ didn't qualify! Paul knew of no exception, so no exception was given.

The apostle then excoriates those who do not take seriously the inspired words of Christ for His church (vv. 4–5). Thus, Scripture itself condemns those who do not take the words of our Lord Jesus Christ—all of them that were given to His disciples—seriously.

Suffice it to say that, when comparing Scripture with Scripture, we come up with the same truths as those found in the Great Commission. The words that Christ gave to His disciples on the Mount of Olives were to be taught to the entire church. *All of them!* Paul demanded it of Timothy. Christ demanded it of His disciples—and He demands it of us today!

One last comment before we leave the Great Commission. At first glance it is easy to miss a certain connection, but when you pick up the line of reasoning in this passage, you will find it in other passages of Scripture as well. Notice that in the Great Commission we are told to "make disciples of all the nations, baptizing them . . . teaching them . . . even to the end of the age." We saw in the previous chapter that "those who endure to the end [of the age] will be saved [delivered] . . . then the end shall come" (Matt. 24:13–14). We are, therefore, as one would expect if the Olivet Discourse is referring to the Rapture, to continue making disciples of all nations, baptizing them and teaching them, right up until the *end of the age.* That is when the true saints of God will be rescued from the wrath of Satan, and when the wrath of God will be poured out upon the wicked who remain. Plain and simple!

In the gospel of John, Christ said,

(39) "And this is the will of Him who sent Me, that of *all that He has given Me I lose nothing but raise it up on the last day.* (40) For this is the will of My Father, that every one who beholds the Son, and believes in Him, may have eternal life; and I myself *will raise him up on the last day*" (John 6:39–40, emphasis added).

The "last day" of what, or before what? The "last day" before the wrath of God begins at the end of the age. That is when we will see the sign of the end of the age. That is when we will see the sign of Christ's coming. And that is when we will see the Son of Man coming with power and great glory to gather together His elect from one end of the sky to the other! Then the wrath of God will begin.

Until then, the Lord commands that we make disciples and teach them to obey everything He has commanded us, and that He will be with us "always, even to the end of the age"!

A Little Test Worth Trying

I would like to give you the same proposition I have given to prophecy classes I have taught over the years. Before they come to any conclusion about which event the Olivet Discourse is referring to, I challenge them to determine for themselves if Christ was referring to the rapture of the saints or to the battle of Armageddon? That assignment has been an effective method of getting the class involved with the text, making them compare Scripture with Scripture in order to have them come up with answers on their own.

Here is the crucial text taken from the Olivet Discourse. Read it carefully for yourself:

> (27) "For just as the lightning comes from the east, and flashes even to the west, so shall the coming [*parousía*] of the Son of Man be. . . . (30) and then the sign of the Son of Man will appear in the sky, and then all the tribes of the earth will mourn, and they will see the Son of Man coming on the clouds of the sky with power and great glory. (31) And He will send forth His angels with a great trumpet and they will gather together His elect from the four winds, from one end of the sky to the other. . . . (37) For the coming [*parousía*] of the Son of Man will be just like the days of Noah. (38) For as in those days which were before the flood they were eating and drinking, they were marrying and giving in marriage, until the day that Noah entered the ark, (39) and they did not understand until the flood came and took them all away; so shall the coming [*parousía*] of the Son of Man be. (40) Then there shall be two men in the field; one will be taken, and one will be left" (Matt. 24:27, 30–31, 37–40).

Now, decide which event Christ had in mind when He gave this specific instruction to His disciples. Does this passage refer to the battle of Armageddon as recorded in Revelation 19:11–21, or does it refer to the rapture of the saints as recorded in 1 Thessalonians 4:15–17? Your very life may one day depend upon your decision, should you be alive when those momentous events begin to unfold. Those prepared in advance have a chance to escape and survive. Those unprepared will have to face, head on, the brunt of Antichrist's ferocious persecution.

It is more than a little significant that, to date, with no exceptions and no fence-sitters, *every* member of *every* class has concluded that this passage describes the rapture of the saints, not the battle of Armageddon. In fact, to date there has yet to be a single vote for the battle of Armageddon! Not a one!

You Can't Have It Both Ways!

Before we leave our defense of the applicability of the Olivet Discourse to the church, let me make one final point. The argument is rather oblique, but I strongly encourage you to use it sometime when you are discussing the timing of the Rapture with your pretrib friends. If nothing else, it will make for interesting discussion.

When the right opportunity presents itself (and I can assure you, it always does), ask your friend if the pretribulation Rapture position permits setting dates as to when the Rapture will occur. He will be adamant that we cannot know "the day or the hour." Perfect! Then ask him how he came to this conclusion. He will invariably quote the verse: "But of that day and hour no one knows, not even the angels of heaven, nor the Son, but the Father alone" (Matt. 24:36). Try it sometime. That's the answer pretribulationists almost always give!

But that answer, although true, presents those holding to the pretribulation view with a serious problem. Why? Because that quotation is taken directly from the Olivet Discourse in Matthew, a passage that those holding to this position make applicable to the battle of Armageddon, not the rapture of God's saints—which they claim happened at least seven years earlier!

You can't have it both ways!

Summing It Up

In summary, I hope I have demonstrated that making the Olivet Discourse inapplicable to the church is a very dangerous position to take. It causes too many contradictions for a serious student of the Bible to overcome without compromising a face-value hermeneutic.

I also hope I have prodded you to compare Scripture with Scripture so that you can decide for yourself whether the Olivet Discourse refers to the battle of Armageddon or to the rapture of God's elect. In my opinion, if you do this carefully, without preconceived assumptions or biases, you can come to only one conclusion: the Olivet Discourse is Christ's teaching about His *parousía*, when He will rapture His elect and destroy the wicked who remain at the end of the age. This was specific instruction given to His disciples—soon to become the founding fathers of the church—to be taught to the new converts who would soon become the body of the church, after His ascension. Just one *parousía* of Christ! Just one Day of the Lord! Just that plain, just that simple!

The Teaching of Paul

It may surprise you to learn that, next to the book of Revelation, the most prophetic books in the New Testament are Paul's two letters to the church at Thessalonica. We have already touched on the classic Rapture passage in 1 Thessalonians 4. Now we will see that in these two great prophetic books Paul makes exactly the same case—and in exactly the same sequence—to the Thessalonian church, the majority of which were Gentiles, that Christ made to His disciples in the Olivet Discourse. In fact, the apostle specifically states that his teaching on end time events comes directly from the Lord Himself. "For this we say to you, by the word of the Lord" (1 Thess. 4:15) is Paul's opening statement, after which he proceeds to give detailed information concerning the rapture of the saints and when it will occur.

If, as argued in the two previous chapters, the Olivet Discourse is referring to the rapture of God's elect, an event that occurs when the sign is given in the sun, moon, and stars announcing the Day of the Lord, then the Rapture Paul instructs the Thessalonian church about, should also occur in connection with the beginning of the Day of the Lord. Follow with me and see for yourself.

The First Letter

Speaking to his readers in Thessalonica, Paul wrote,

> (13) But we do not want you to be uninformed, brethren, about those who are asleep, that you may not grieve, as do the rest who have no hope. (14) For if we believe that Jesus died and rose again, even so God will bring with Him those who have fallen asleep in Jesus (1 THESS. 4:13–14).

Paul understood the concerns the Thessalonians had about their deceased friends and relatives who had professed Christ when they were living. Their question was the same one we have all asked at some time in our life: "What happens to those who have died before us?" So Paul now explains that those who have "fallen asleep [have died] in Jesus" are not without hope, and in the next four verses the apostle explains why there is hope.

The Classic Rapture Passage

As we saw in the previous chapter, these verses are considered the classic Rapture passage of the Bible:

> (15) For this we say to you by the word of the Lord, that we who are alive, and remain until the coming [*parousía*] of the Lord, shall not precede those who have fallen asleep. (16) For the Lord Himself will descend from heaven with a shout, with the voice of the archangel, and with the trumpet of God; and the dead in Christ shall rise first. (17) Then we who are alive and remain shall be caught up together with them in the clouds to meet the Lord in the air, and thus we shall always be with the Lord. (18) Therefore comfort one another with these words (1 THESS. 4:15–18).

The message of this passage is self-explanatory. The church at Thessalonica was told not to worry about those who had already died, because when Christ comes to rapture the living believers, He will first resurrect those who have died "in Jesus." Then both the living and the dead believers will be caught up together in the clouds to meet the Lord in the air.

The Day of the Lord Connection

Paul's instruction continues on into the fifth chapter, and it is extremely easy to follow his line of thought. The Thessalonians had just been introduced to the *parousía* of Christ, when the saints will be caught up to meet the Lord in the air. Although not specifically stated, the logical question in any person's mind would be, "When?"—the same question the disciples expressed to Christ at the beginning of the Olivet Discourse, and the same question still being asked today. In reality, that question is the basis upon which this book has been written.

Therefore, even before the question could even be asked, Paul gives the believers in Thessalonica their answer:

(1) *Now as to the times and the epochs, brethren, you have no need of anything to be written to you.* (2) For you yourselves know full well that *the day of the Lord* will come just like a thief in the night. (3) While they are saying, "Peace and safety!" then destruction will come upon them suddenly like birth pangs upon a woman with child; and they shall not escape (1 THESS. 5:1–3, emphasis added).

When will the Rapture occur? They should already know, Paul says. *The Rapture will take place when the Day of the Lord begins!* Nothing needs to be written to them concerning the times and epochs (better translated "seasons," KJV) when this great event will occur.

Obviously, in light of this comment, this is not the first time Paul has discussed the timing of the Rapture with them. In his second letter to them, written a short time later, he again reminds them that he is repeating things he has already told them, things not a part of this first letter to them. Although this is only a guess on my part, because Paul's instruction here parallels what Christ taught His disciples, it would seem probable that the Olivet Discourse had been the topic of an earlier conversation with them. This is why Paul tells them that his instruction to them is "by the word of the Lord" (1 Thess. 4:15).

In the Olivet Discourse, Christ had explained that His angels would gather together the elect of God from one end of the sky to the other when the sign of the end of the age, the day of the Lord's wrath, was given in the sun, moon, and stars (see Matt. 24:29–31; cf. Joel 2:31). In like manner, Paul instructs the Thessalonians that the time and season in which we, who are alive, will be caught up to meet the Lord in the air—the Rapture—will be when the Day of the Lord comes. The end of the age and the Day of the Lord are one and the same event, when God promises to gather together His elect to meet the Lord in the air, before Christ destroys the wicked who remain on earth. The parallel of Paul's teaching to Christ's Olivet Discourse is overwhelming! In both, the elect are "gathered together" or "caught up together" before the wrath of God begins.

Because of the implications that can be made by tying the Rapture to the Day of the Lord, not unlike the concerns discussed in chapter 3 (the last point that shows that the Rapture and the initiation of God's wrath occur on the same day), some would have you believe that Paul's instruction on the Day of the Lord in chapter 5 has no bearing on his instruction on the Rapture introduced in chapter 4. They will tell you that Paul is talking about two completely separate end time events, and that the chapter division separates his instruction on the Rapture from his instruction on the Day of the Lord.

However, the original Greek manuscripts of the New Testament contained no chapters, paragraphs, or verses. These were added over a thousand years later. Therefore, students of God's Word must not be misled by where a chapter or verse ends in our English translations; rather, we must study a passage in its context, taking into consideration where the thought begins and where it ends.

In this instance, in 4:13, Paul tells the Thessalonians that he does not want them to be "uninformed . . . about those who are asleep." However, his discussion of this issue is not finished at the end of chapter 4, for Paul actually concludes his thoughts on the matter when he finishes informing his brethren in 5:10 "that whether we are awake or asleep, we may live together with Him." Plainly, then, this passage concerning the times and seasons when the Day of the Lord will occur is directly connected to the verses immediately preceding, which speak directly to the rapture of the saints at the *parousía* of Christ. It does not refer to a new, completely unrelated issue. Rather, it refers to the interrelationship of these two critical end time events—the Rapture and God's wrath—teaching exactly the same thing that Christ taught in the Olivet Discourse. The end of the fourth chapter tells us that the Rapture will occur at the coming (*parousía*) of Christ; the beginning of the fifth chapter tells us that His coming will occur when the Day of the Lord commences, and verses 10 and 11 of chapter 5 finish the thought begun back in chapter 4, verse 13. Thus, those two back-to-back events described by Paul parallel the two back-to-back signs described by Christ—the sign of His *parousía* and of the end of the age.

Paul goes on to say,

(4) But *you*, brethren, are not in darkness, that the day [of the Lord] should overtake *you* like a thief; (5) for *you* are all sons of light and sons of day. *We* are not of night nor of darkness; (6) so then let us not sleep as others do, but let *us* be alert and sober. (7)

For those who sleep do their sleeping at night, and those who get drunk get drunk at night. (8) But since *we* are of the day, let *us* be sober, having put on the breastplate of faith and love, and as a helmet, the hope of salvation [deliverance]. (9) *For God has not destined us for wrath, but for obtaining salvation* [deliverance] through our Lord Jesus Christ, (10) who died for *us, that whether we are awake or asleep, we may live together with Him.* (11) Therefore encourage one another, and build up one another, just as you also are doing (1 THESS. 5:4–11, emphasis added).

Paul tells the Thessalonian church that they are to be alert and sober so that this day will not overtake them like a thief! Why? Because *you*—genuine believers—are of the light and not of the darkness. Because "God has not destined us for wrath [the Day of the Lord], but for obtaining salvation [deliverance—*sōtēría*]" (v. 9).

Earlier, we looked at the verb form of the Greek word *sōtēría*, which can refer to either spiritual salvation or physical deliverance (see chapter 4). Here, as was the case in the Olivet Discourse, Paul is addressing believing Thessalonians who are already spiritually saved. And, like Christ, Paul uses the identical Greek word. Therefore, like Christ, he has to be referring to their *physical* deliverance—to the rapture of the saints that he has just described to them a few verses earlier—once again neatly pulling together these two critical end time events, the Rapture and God's wrath.

Summing Up the First Letter

In summary, then, we see that the critical part of Paul's teaching in his first letter to the Thessalonians concerns the *parousía* of Christ, when the saints "shall be caught up together . . . to meet the Lord in the air," and the interrelationship of His coming to rapture His saints to the Day of the Lord. We also see that Paul's teaching concerning the Rapture precisely parallels the same two issues the disciples questioned Christ about: "What will be the sign of your coming [*parousía*], and of the end of the age [the Day of the Lord]," when your angels "will gather together His elect from the four winds, from one end of the sky to the other"? In addition, certain critical Greek words relating to end time events are used in both passages (i.e., *parousía, sōtería,* etc.). Is it any wonder that Paul begins his instruction by telling the Thessalonians that he speaks "by the word of the Lord"?

If Paul's teaching parallels the teaching of Christ, then the Olivet Discourse must be a reference to the Rapture, not to the battle of Armageddon. And if that is the case, then the Rapture will cut short the persecution by Antichrist immediately after the sign of the Day of the Lord is given in the sun, moon, and stars, plain and simple!

The Second Letter

Paul's second letter to the Thessalonian church thoroughly substantiates the sequence of events given in the Olivet Discourse that must occur before the coming of Christ, when Christ will rescue the saints from Antichrist's persecution and then destroy the wicked who remain during the Day of the Lord. Because this is such a significant passage, however, I find myself caught between the proverbial rock and a hard place. Let me explain.

Help!

In this particular passage, the Greek is more precise than the English translation. So if I argue this critical text from the English translation alone, scholars who want to attack the prewrath position as argued in this book will tell you that I don't know what I'm talking about because I don't have an expert's working knowledge of the original language underlying this important text. And indeed, they would have every right to say that if that was the approach I decided to take. On the other hand, if I argue from the Greek text, the layperson is likely to say that now I'm the one playing games with Scripture, getting the passage to say what I want it to say rather than simply letting the text speak for itself as translated into English. And while it is true that some play games with the English text, using their knowledge of the Greek to convince the listener of something other than what appears obvious in a good translation, may God help me if I ever do that intentionally! I simply want to find the truth, and for that reason, I have tried to get as close to the original text as I could in order to be faithful to the true intent of the passage being studied. That is the only approach I can take if I truly want to have integrity when it comes to understanding what an important text like this is trying to say.

I have sought aid from Dr. Scott Carroll, a man who has a passion for the Word of God and who, in addition, reads twelve ancient languages. One of these languages is Greek, which he has studied and taught for many years. I have had Scott, as well as several of his colleagues, double-check every use of the Greek in this book, giving me their guidance and understanding as to what the underlying text is trying to convey to the reader. They have checked every word and nuance, every jot and tittle of what I have written. They even dictated explanations that were in keeping with the original text. And when I have taken exception with the English translation, it has been done only as a result of the best scholarship available to me.

Now, with this in mind let's continue with Paul's all-important second letter to the church at Thessalonica.

The Context

A short time after the apostle wrote his first letter to the Thessalonians, a crisis arose in their church, one that touched directly on the teaching we have just looked at in his first letter. False teachers had come into the congregation and had taught the Thessalonians, who were then undergoing severe persecution, that the Day of the Lord was already in process. Whether these false teachers were implying that there would be no deliverance (i.e., rapture) of the righteous now that the

Day of the Lord's wrath had begun, or whether they were simply implying that the Thessalonians were not genuinely saved and therefore had missed the Rapture altogether, is not clear from the text. Either way, their teaching was false, and if the Thessalonian church had remembered Paul's teaching in his first letter, the problem could have been avoided.

The false teaching to which they had been exposed directly contradicted the apostle's earlier instruction to them that "God has not destined us for wrath, but for obtaining salvation [deliverance]" (1 Thess. 5:9) and that they would be "caught up together . . . to meet the Lord in the air" (4:17) *before* the wrath of God was poured out upon the wicked world that remains at the Day of the Lord (5:1–2). Wanting to encourage them, the apostle said,

> (4) We ourselves speak proudly of you among the churches of God *for your perseverance and faith in the midst of all your persecutions and afflictions which you endure.* (5) This is a plain indication of God's righteous judgment so that you may be considered worthy of the kingdom of God, for which indeed you are suffering. (6) For after all *it is only just for God to repay with affliction those who afflict you,* (7) *and to give relief to you who are afflicted and to us as well when the Lord Jesus shall be revealed from heaven with His mighty angels in flaming fire,* (8) *dealing out retribution to those who do not know God* and to those who do not obey the gospel of our Lord Jesus. . . . (11) To this end also we pray for you always that our God may count you worthy of your calling . . . (2 THESS. 1:4–8, 11, emphasis added).

If you carefully trace the sequence of events in the passage quoted above, you will quickly realize that it again parallels the sequence that Christ taught His disciples in His Olivet Discourse.

First, the persecution—"in the midst of all your persecutions."

Then, cutting short that time of persecution by the deliverance or rescue of the elect (the Rapture)—"to give relief[1] to you who are afflicted and to us as well."

Followed by the fiery wrath of God—"when the Lord Jesus shall be revealed from heaven with His mighty angels in flaming fire, dealing out retribution to those who do not know God."

Clearly and precisely, Paul tells them again what he had taught them in his first letter: God will "give relief to you who are afflicted" when "Jesus is revealed from heaven with His mighty angels in flaming fire." In other words, the faithful will be rescued—given relief—from persecution *before* the wrath of God is poured out upon the wicked during the Day of the Lord.

Therefore, the persecution they were then undergoing *could not be* the wrath of God! Rather, Paul reminds them that God will "repay with affliction, those who afflict you" (2 Thess. 1:6). In other words, God's wrath will not be poured out upon "you"— the church at Thessalonica—but upon those who are tormenting "you"! To those of you who have been afflicted, he will give relief. It is interesting to note that the Greek verb used here, translated "afflict," comes from the same Greek root as the noun *thlípsis*, which is the identical word translated "tribulation" or "persecution" in the Olivet Discourse (Matt. 24:9, 21). Once again, understanding the precise Greek language pulls the two parallel passages and thoughts together nicely.

1. It is interesting to note that the word translated "relief" in this particular text comes from the Greek word *ánesis*, which occurs only four other times in the New Testament. Like any word, *ánesis* has shades of meaning that we learn from its use both in and outside sacred literature. Meanings range from "relief," to "set free," to "give up," or even to "take up." The best meaning is always ruled by the immediate context. While *relief* makes a nice contrast to the affliction being referred to here in this passage, *ánesis* is not being contrasted with the affliction, but rather, the Greek shows that the *ánesis* and God's wrath will both occur at the revelation of Christ. If we choose to translate *ánesis* from the perspective of "taking up" those who are afflicted at the revelation of Christ, the Rapture and God's wrath are once again beautifully tied together at the coming of Christ by the specific Greek words Paul chose to use in this text.

The New Problem

Paul then deals more specifically with the problem at hand. The church at Thessalonica had obviously forgotten the things that were to happen *before* those two back-to-back events—the Rapture and God's wrath—could take place at Christ's coming (*parousía*). Had they remembered the Olivet Discourse (which I believe they were familiar with) or had they remembered Paul's previous personal instruction to them (which obviously they hadn't) they would never have believed the false teachers. Good doctrine, when rightly understood and rightly applied, always prevents problems. As it was, Paul had to instruct them again.

Follow carefully what the apostle says:

(1) *Now we request you, brethren, with regard to the coming [parousía] of our Lord Jesus Christ, and our gathering together to Him,* (2) that you may not be quickly shaken from your composure or be disturbed either by a spirit or a message or a letter as if from us, *to the effect that the day of the Lord has come* (2 THESS. 2:1–2, emphasis added).

Paul begins in chapter 2 by encouraging the Thessalonians that they should have bedrock confidence ("that you may not be quickly shaken from your composure") in the coming (*parousía*) of Christ and our gathering together to Him. That's the idea conveyed in the original Greek.

Notice how Paul again neatly ties this "gathering together to Him [Christ]" at "the coming [*parousía*] of our Lord Jesus Christ" to "the day of the Lord" (vv. 1–2)!

False teaching had perverted this truth, and Paul makes it clear that this false teaching—that the Day of the Lord was already in process—had not originated from him. They were not to be disturbed "to the effect that the day of the Lord has come" (v. 2).[2] It was not true, and it directly contradicted what Paul had taught them previously.

The Sequence of End Time Events

Just as Christ had done some twenty years earlier for His disciples, Paul now carefully outlines the sequence of events that must occur prior to the coming (*parousía*) of Christ, when the saints will be gathered together to Him and the wrath of God will descend upon those who remain.

(3) Let no one in any way deceive you, for it [the Day of the Lord] will not come unless *the apostasy comes first, and the man of lawlessness is revealed,* the son of destruction, (4) who opposes and exalts himself above every so-called god or object of worship, *so that he takes his seat in the temple of God, displaying himself as being God* (2 THESS. 2:3–4, emphasis added).

To begin with, Paul tells them not to be deceived by these false teachers. Before the Day of the Lord can commence, certain other events have to occur. *First,* they must see the apostasy, and *then,* the revealing of the man of lawlessness (v. 3), who will take his seat in the temple, displaying himself as being God (v. 4b).[3]

2. The Greek verb "has come" is in the perfect indicative tense, which means the subject—in this case, "the Day of the Lord"—is in the process of happening, rather than having already begun and ended. The Greek perfect tense focuses on the present results of a past act.

3. The question revolves around what is meant by the phrase "comes first." Although the translation suggests that the apostasy is the first event in the sequence given in the sentence itself, the revealing of Antichrist becoming the second event, taking his seat in the temple the third, etc., in reality the *Greek grammar used in this text demands* that Paul in verses 3–4 is not trying to establish a strict sequence of events that must occur in relationship to one another; rather, he is telling the Thessalonians what events must occur *first,* before the Day of the Lord mentioned in verse 2 can occur. The Greek construction shows that the apostasy and the revealing of Antichrist who takes his seat in the temple are a single event, occurring simultaneously; it is this singular, first event (i.e., the apostasy that is associated directly with the man of lawlessness, when he takes his seat in the temple and demands the worship of the world) that must occur *first,* before the second event, the Day of the Lord, can actually begin.

The Apostasy Comes First

It is obvious from the context that the Thessalonians had not seen either of these events happen, because Paul is telling them that the persecution they are undergoing cannot be, by definition, the Day of the Lord, "for it will not come unless the apostasy comes first."

With proper Greek construction in mind (see footnote 3), and comparing Scripture with Scripture, we find that *"the* apostasy" referred to here must be the same apostasy that Christ warned His disciples about in the Olivet Discourse:

(9) "Then they will deliver you to tribulation, and will kill you, and you will be hated by all nations on account of My name. (10) *And at that time many will fall away* and will deliver up one another and hate one another. (11) And many false prophets will arise, and will mislead many. (12) And because lawlessness is increased, *most people's love* [for Christ] *will grow cold.* (13) *But the one who endures to the end, he shall be saved* [delivered]" (Matt. 24:9–13, emphasis added).

The only apostasy directly referred to in the Bible that occurs simultaneously with Antichrist's spectacular rise to power at the midpoint of the tribulation period, is the "falling away" that Christ describes in the Olivet Discourse. To "fall away" is precisely what the word *apostasy* means. However, some people have tried to tie the apostasy referred to here by Paul, to the general apostasy of the world described in 2 Timothy 3:1–5 that comes in the last days *before* the specific apostasy of the church in general, which Christ associates with Antichrist's persecution. If that is the case, they argue, then Christ's coming could still occur before the tribulation period ever begins.

Which apostasy Paul is referring to, the general or the specific, really makes no difference to his argument as to the sequence of events that must occur prior to Christ's coming at the

Day of the Lord. Either way, the man of sin must be revealed, taking his seat in the temple and demanding the worship of the world, before the "coming of our Lord Jesus Christ, and our gathering together to Him" (2 Thess. 2:1) can occur.

However, I do not think that the general apostasy referred to in 2 Timothy is the same apostasy discussed in 2 Thessalonians—for at least two reasons.

First, the apostasy referred to in 2 Thessalonians 2:3 is *the* apostasy (a definite article before "apostasy"), indicating a very specific apostasy the Thessalonians already knew about. And the only apostasy they could have known about was the apostasy that Christ directly associated with His coming (*parousía*) in the Olivet Discourse. Therefore, it doesn't take any stretch of the imagination to see that *the falling away* described in the Olivet Discourse is *the apostasy* (which, remember, means "a falling away") described in 2 Thessalonians, especially in light of the fact that Paul spoke concerning end time events "by the word of the Lord"!

Second, and equally important, Paul's second letter to Timothy, which describes the general apostasy of the world that comes in the last days, was written about fifteen years after Paul's second letter to the Thessalonians. Therefore, it's hard to refer to something that has meaning to the readers, if that something isn't revealed until fifteen years later.

Antichrist Revealed in the Temple

Now back to our text. Paul tells the confused Thessalonians that certain events must occur *before* the *parousía* of Christ can initiate the great day of God's wrath. The Day of the Lord can only occur *after* Antichrist, the man of lawlessness, has been revealed and has taken his seat in the temple at the midpoint of the final seven-year tribulation period, demanding the worship of the world (paralleling Matt. 24:15; cf. Rev. 13:4–8); and *after* the falling away—the apostasy—of many who profess the name of Christ (paralleling Matt. 24:9–12). Then Paul continues his instruction by asking,

> Do you not remember that while I was still with you, I was telling you these things? (2 THESS. 2:5).

Obviously, he must have explained these events in a previous conversation not recorded in Scripture, because there is no mention of this specific sequence of events in his first letter. Most likely, as we saw when working through Paul's first letter to the Thessalonians, he'd had an earlier discussion with them about the Olivet Discourse of Christ. Now that a question had arisen as to when the Day of the Lord would actually begin, he refers again to this face-to-face conversation he had already had with them.

The Restrainer Removed

In the next two verses, Paul reminds the Thessalonians:

> (6) And you know what restrains him [Antichrist] now, so that in his time he [Antichrist] may be revealed. (7) For the mystery of lawlessness is already at work; only he who now restrains will do so until he is taken out of the way (2 THESS. 2:6–7).

Here, Paul simply makes the point that all of these events that must occur before the Day of the Lord can begin cannot occur until the restrainer is first removed. Only then will Antichrist be revealed as the monster he really is, demanding the worship of the world from the temple in Jerusalem.

When Paul says "you know," he is again referring to the previous instruction he has given them, in this case instruction about "he who now restrains." When it comes to the identity of the restrainer, we know only what is recorded here, which is not as much as we would like, and his identity has long been hotly debated—*although who the restrainer is has little to do with the sequence of events Paul is giving here.*

Those who expect the church to be gone before Antichrist's persecution begins (namely, the pretribulationists) do all that they can to make the restrainer someone or something that removes the church before the persecution at the hands of Antichrist begins. For that reason, before we continue with Paul's instruction to the Thessalonians, let us look briefly at the options that are given us as to the identity of the restrainer. I believe that when Scripture is compared to Scripture, certain possibilities can be quickly eliminated. However, we will also look at one possibility that I think every serious student of God's Word should not dismiss so quickly.

Who, then, is the restrainer to whom Paul refers? Is it the true church? The Holy Spirit? Human government? Who?

The Thessalonian text does not say. But the Greek noun *ekklēsía* ("church") is feminine, and "restrainer" in verse 7 is masculine, which rules out the church. More important, however, the context of Paul's second letter to the Thessalonians is his instruction about what must happen *before* Christ comes to rapture His saints at the Day of the Lord (2 Thess. 2:1–2), making the true church of Christ an impossible candidate for the restrainer. You can't make the removal of the saints a condition that must be met before the saints are removed and the Day of the Lord begins, can you? Somehow the logic of that circular reasoning escapes me.

Other pretribulationists will assert that the restrainer is the Holy Spirit, reasoning that because the Holy Spirit indwells the true believer, the removal of the restrainer is an indirect reference to the rapture of the saints. But again, the circular reasoning that makes the true church an impossible candidate for the restrainer also makes the Holy Spirit an impossible candidate. Furthermore, like the elect of God, the Holy Spirit will still be on earth *after* Antichrist begins his persecution of the elect (Mark 13:11; cf. Matt. 24:21–22, 31).

Finally, some interpreters believe the restrainer is human government. But human government clearly continues under the rule of Antichrist after his true identity is revealed (Rev. 17:12), making that option also unacceptable. If Paul had been referring to the church, the Holy Spirit, or human government, why wouldn't he have said precisely that? Perhaps the reason is that the restrainer is indeed *the restrainer* referred to in the Old Testament. Which leads me to the candidate I believe is a real possibility.

I think a strong case can be made for the restrainer being the archangel Michael. We learn from the prophet Daniel that Michael's work is to "stand firmly against" or "restrain" the forces of evil (Dan. 10:21), and we are later told that Michael will "arise" or "stand still" (Dan. 12:1; the Hebrew verb *amad* can mean either) just prior to the great persecution of Antichrist. The idea in the Hebrew text is that Michael, "who stands guard over the sons of your people," must remove his protection—arise, stand still—before "there will be a time of distress such as never occurred since there was a nation until that time" (Dan. 12:1).

That passage parallels the present 2 Thessalonians passage, where we are told that the restrainer "is taken out of the way" before "the lawless one" is revealed (2:7–8). Thus, Satan is not able to afflict Israel or the elect of God to the degree he desires until God removes the angelic protection of Michael. Only then can Antichrist have access to those who claim the name of Christ, to test the genuineness of their faith. (More will be said about this in the next two chapters.)

However, as already noted, the identity of the restrainer does not affect the sequence of events that must occur before Christ comes. We only know that he must be removed before Antichrist can be revealed, and that Antichrist must be revealed before the events described in verse 8 can occur.

The Appearance of His Coming

We are now ready to look at the most significant verse in this passage concerning the timing of Christ's parousía *that initiates the Day of the Lord.* In his first letter, Paul had already told the Thessalonians that God had promised that true believers would never undergo His wrath, that the rapture of the true children of God would occur just before the Day of the Lord began. So now, Paul reminds them that *before* God's wrath will come, the church will undergo "*the* apostasy," when "the man of lawlessness is revealed . . . so that he takes his seat in the temple of God, displaying himself as being God" (2 Thess. 2:3–4). Summing it up, Paul tells them that

> (7b) he who now restrains will do so until he is taken out of the way. (8) And *then that lawless one will be revealed whom the Lord will* slay with the breath of His mouth and *bring to an end* [render useless][4] *by the appearance of His coming* [parousía] (2 THESS. 2:7–8, emphasis added).

Note carefully what this text is saying. It is vital to our determination of the precise timing of Christ's coming, when He will gather together His elect and begin His wrath on those who remain.

In the same manner that Christ taught His disciples He would "cut short" the persecution by Antichrist when those persecuted are delivered (i.e., raptured)—immediately following the two back-to-back signs that will be given in the heavens at His *parousía*—so likewise Paul tells the confused Thessalonians that He will "bring to an end [the lawless one] by the *appearance* of Christ's coming [parousía]!" In both accounts, before Christ's *parousía* can occur, Antichrist must be on the scene, in "his seat in the temple of God, displaying himself as being God"

---

4. To "bring to an end" translates the Greek word *kataregō*, which means to "render useless" or "paralyze."

(2 Thess. 2:4; cf. Matt. 24:15). It will be the *appearance* of Christ's *parousía* that will initiate the Day of the Lord's judgment upon Antichrist! It will be the *appearance* of Christ's *parousía* when the faithful will be gathered together to Christ. Therefore, the Thessalonian church need not be deceived concerning "the coming [*parousía*] of our Lord Jesus Christ, and our gathering together to Him . . . to the effect that the day of the Lord has come" (2 Thess. 2:1–2). It can't occur until all of these other things happen first! Just that plain. Just that simple.

Summing Up Both Letters

To sum up the instruction of Paul to the Thessalonians, let us compare his teaching with the teaching of Christ to His disciples in the Olivet Discourse:

Both accounts give the direct instruction of Christ (Matt. 24:3–4a; cf. 1 Thess. 4:15).

Both accounts begin with a severe warning to Christians about what is being taught (Matt. 24:4; cf. 2 Thess. 2:3).

Both accounts refer to the coming (*parousía*) of Christ (Matt. 24:3, 27, 37, 39; cf. 1 Thess. 4:15; 2 Thess. 2:1, 8).

Both accounts connect the Day of the Lord with the coming of Christ (Matt. 24:3, 29 30, 37 39; cf. 1 Thess. 4:15–5:2; 2 Thess. 2:1–2).

Both accounts refer to the revealing of Antichrist, which will occur in the temple, in the holy place (Matt. 24:15; cf. 2 Thess. 2:4).

Both accounts make reference to *the* apostasy, the specific falling away that occurs when Antichrist is revealed, demanding the worship of the world (Matt. 24:9–12; cf. 2 Thess. 2:3–4).

Both accounts teach that at Christ's coming (*parousía*) He will "cut short" or "bring to an end"—render useless—the hostile activities of Antichrist (Matt. 24:22; cf. 2 Thess. 2:8).

COMPARATIVE ACCOUNTS

The Olivet Discourse (Matt. 24) and the Books of I & II Thessalonians

The Olivet Discourse of Christ		The Instruction of Paul
24:3-4a	THE SOURCE OF THE INSTRUCTION IS CHRIST	I Th 4:15
24:4b	THE WARNING CONCERNING THE INSTRUCTION	II Th 2:3
24:3, 27 24:37, 39	THE SUBJECT MATTER: CHRIST'S PAROUSIA	I Th 4:15 II Th 2:3 II Th 2:8
24:3, 29-30 24:37-39	CHRIST'S PAROUSIA INITIATES GOD'S JUDGMENT	I Th 5:1-3 II Th 2:1-2
24:15	ANTICHRIST'S TEMPLE DEBUT	II Th 2:4b
24:9, 21	PERSECUTION (OPPOSITION) BY ANTICHRIST	II Th 2:3-4a
24:9-12	THE APOSTASY OF THE CHURCH	II Th 2:3
24:22, 29-30	CHRIST'S PAROUSIA CUTS SHORT (ENDS) PERSECUTION	II Th 2:8
24:31	THE GATHERING (RAPTURE) OF GOD'S ELECT	I Th 4:15-17 II Th 2:1
24:14, 37-39	THE WRATH OF GOD (THE DAY OF THE LORD)	I Th 5:1-3

Both accounts teach that at Christ's coming (*parousía*) the day of the Lord's wrath will begin (Matt. 24:29–30, 36–39; cf. 1 Thess. 5:1–2; 2 Thess. 2:1–2; cf. v. 8).

Both accounts teach that when the Day of the Lord begins, God's elect, His saints, will be gathered together (Matt. 24:31; cf. 1 Thess. 4:17–5:2; 2 Thess. 2:1–2).

The account in Matthew tells us *who* does the gathering: "His [Christ's] angels" (Matt. 24:31); Paul's first account tells us *where* and to *whom* we will be gathered: "in the clouds to meet the Lord in the air" (1 Thess. 4:17); and Paul's second letter tells us *when*: "at the appearance of His coming [*parousía*]" (2 Thess. 2:8); and all three passages connect this great event—the rapture of the church—with another awesome event, the Day of the Lord (Matt. 24:3, 29, 37–39; 1 Thess. 5:1–3; 2 Thess. 2:1–2), bringing all three accounts into proper perspective and relationship to one another concerning the great hope of the true church of Christ and the wrath of God that awaits the children of Satan.

Between the wrath of Satan and the wrath of God, the elect will be rescued. The rapture of God's saints. Identical messages! Identical timing! Taught by Christ and confirmed by Paul. That is the prewrath Rapture position, plain and simple.

One Last Warning

Before we leave Paul's second letter to the Thessalonians, we need to look briefly at a warning at the very end of the book. When Christ taught His disciples the order of events that must occur before His coming (*parousía*), He prefaced those remarks with the warning, "See to it that no one misleads you" (Matt. 24:4). When Paul taught the church of Thessalonica the same order of events, he also prefaced his remarks with the warning, "Let no one in any way deceive you" (2 Thess. 2:3). Then, at the very end of that second letter (2 Thess. 3:14–15),

Paul gives one last warning that most refuse to deal with in its proper context.

Many will tell you that this final warning was given to those living unruly lives, as mentioned earlier in the chapter (vv. 11–12). But the intervening verse 13 changes the direction of the thought, and the language of verse 14 refers to the overall "instruction in this letter," not to the side issue of undisciplined living to which Paul devotes only two verses.

The main objective of Paul's second letter to the Thessalonians was to put an end to the confusion that existed in the church about the return of Christ for His saints by clarifying the sequence of end time events that must occur before Christ's *parousía*. He prefaces his instruction with the admonition, "Let no one in any way deceive you" (2 Thess. 2:3). Then, at the end of the letter, Paul gives a final warning:

> (14) If anyone does not obey our instruction in this letter, take special note of that man and do not associate with him, so that he may be put to shame. (15) And yet do not regard him [a Christian who refuses to accept Paul's instruction about the last days] as an enemy, but admonish him as a brother" (2 THESS. 3:14–15).

Most of us can live with verse 15; it's verse 14 that we would prefer to overlook. You will need to decide for yourself exactly what that final warning is saying, but in my opinion, given its context, the meaning is quite clear. It is not unlike the passage we looked at earlier from 1 Timothy 6:3–4, where Paul warns Timothy concerning those who don't agree with the sound words of our Lord Jesus Christ and are advocating a different doctrine. In both cases, Paul gives a stern warning concerning those who teach something other than what is clearly taught, especially when, for any reason, the words of Christ to His disciples are made inapplicable to the church!

Both of these admonitions caution true believers about the same things, and obviously God put them there for a reason.

To be forewarned is to be forearmed. Because the stakes are so high, your view of end times may determine whether you, your children, or your grandchildren survive the onslaught of Antichrist or die at his hands if someday you have to face this "great tribulation [persecution], such as has not occurred since the beginning of the world until now, nor ever shall" (Matt. 24:21)!

7

The Teaching
of Revelation

The book of Revelation gives more detail about end time events than any other book in the Bible. Although those of you reading this may be the exception because of your interest in prophetic issues, most Christians don't spend a lot of time studying Revelation. Some are convinced that what the book has to teach is not really that important to the church in general or to genuine bond-servants of Christ, in particular. Pretribulationists, for example, believe that true Christians will be raptured before the trouble described in Revelation ever begins. Because they equate the wrath of Satan with the wrath of God, they teach that the true church will be removed before the commencement of the events that begin in the sixth chapter of Revelation. As evidence they point to the fact that the word *church* is not used from the end of chapter 3 until near the very end of the book, in chapter 22. Therefore, their argument goes, if the word *church* is not used in any of the critical chapters that describe the events of this final seven-year tribulation period (chapters 6–19), then the church must have already been removed (i.e., raptured).

But be careful at this point. The fact that the word *church* is not used in the heart of the book only validates once again the fact that *it will not be the church in general* that undergoes Antichrist's persecution. On the contrary, *it will be the faithful remnant within the church* that will stand true to Christ during these difficult times.

It is also interesting and significant to note that John, the recorder of the book of Revelation, also penned the gospel of John and the epistle of 1 John. He doesn't use the word *church* in either of those books. In addition, the word *church* is never used in the three classic Rapture passages referred to by pretribulationists—1 Thessalonians 4:13–17; 1 Corinthians 15:51–53; or John 14:1–3. Also, except for general references in the first verses of 1 and 2 Thessalonians, neither of those two great prophetic books uses the word *church* either.

As we have already worked through in some depth, when the real trouble begins, the "hard labor" so to speak, the church in general will fall away from the faith—the apostasy—when most people's love for Christ will grow cold. Therefore, it will not be the church in general that stands firm for Christ, but only the true believers (i.e., the saints, overcomers, bond-servants, elect of God) will "endure to the end" through the difficult events detailed in the heart of the book of Revelation, before the great persecution by Antichrist is cut short by the events associated with the sign given in the sun, moon, and stars. For that reason, John uses the word *saint* to depict the genuine bond-servant of Christ, not the word *church*. That is why the word *saint* is used thirteen times in the heart of the book (see 5:8; 8:3–4; 11:18; 13:7, 10; 14:12; 16:6; 17:6; 18:20, 24; 19:8; 20:9), and the word *church* is avoided altogether!

In fact, the book of Revelation isn't even addressed to the church in general, but to the true bond-servants of Christ. It is "the revelation of Jesus Christ, which God gave Him [Christ] to show to His bond-servants" (1:1). Revelation does, however, contain severe warnings to seven specific churches about what will happen to them when the adversity hits. But even then, in each instance, Christ separates those "who have ears to hear"—genuine bond-servants of Christ who listen carefully to what the Spirit is telling these churches—from the specific church that He is reprimanding.

John not only tells us that the book of Revelation is written for the bond-servants of Christ, but he goes on to exhort us concerning the importance of understanding what the book is teaching:

> Blessed is he who reads and those who hear the words of the prophecy, and heed the things written in it . . . (REV. 1:3).

This admonition to Christ's bond-servants pertains to more than just the first and final three chapters of the book. The true bond-servant should not only know what the book is saying, but should *heed* what it says as well! What need would there be to warn the bond-servants to heed the instruction of this book if they were never in any danger to begin with? It makes no sense!

But as we continue, the relevance of the book of Revelation to every genuine believer will become even more obvious, especially when we let the Olivet Discourse interpret the book for us. However, before we look at the critical chapters that parallel the teachings of Christ and Paul, there are several general considerations that will be helpful for you to remember while studying the book.

Did you know that the book of Revelation is not the revelation of John, the writer of the book, but rather, the revelation of Jesus Christ Himself (1:1)? This is important, because Christ cannot contradict Himself. If the teaching of Christ in the Olivet Discourse deals with end times, and the revelation of Christ as recorded in the book of Revelation also deals with end time events, the two accounts should parallel one another . . . and they do.

Did you know that the book of Revelation is the final book of the Bible—both in sequence and in date of authorship—and as such pulls together and shows the completion of the promises given both to the nation of Israel in the Old Testament and to the church in the New Testament? Just as the first eleven chapters of Genesis are the foundational chapters of the entire Bible, for Jews and Gentiles alike, so the book of Revelation is the summation of the Scriptures for Jews and Gentiles alike.

Did you know that the theme of the book of Revelation is wrath? That it describes, in detail, the wrath of Satan (12:12) and the wrath of God (6:16–17), and that to understand Revelation, we must understand which is which?

Did you know that the ancient scrolls normally had their seals on the outside of the scroll, and that when the scroll had legal significance, the seals represented conditions that had to be met before the scroll could be opened? That, in like manner, there are conditions that must be met before God's wrath can commence? That the wrath of God will not begin until all seven seals on the heavenly scroll have been broken and the scroll can be opened?

And, finally, did you know that in the same manner in which Christ warned His disciples not to be misled (Matt. 24:4), and Paul warned the Thessalonians not to be deceived (2 Thess. 2:3), Christ also warns John of the seriousness of the book of Revelation, saying, "If anyone takes away from the words of the book of this prophecy, God shall take away his part from the tree of life and from the holy city, which are written in this book" (Rev. 22:19)?

All right. Enough "did you knows." As I hope you have come to realize, the book of Revelation is a very important book for every Christian to read and heed. It is Christ's revelation to His disciple John, written for the true bond-servants of Christ, not for the church in general. (Those warnings were limited to chapters 2 and 3.) What it says must not be tampered with, including chapters 4 to 19! To do so has dire consequences. Remember, the underlying theme of the book is wrath: Satan's wrath and God's wrath, never to be confused or interchanged with one another.

The Context

In Revelation 5, the angel asks

with a loud voice, "Who is worthy to open the book [the scroll with its seven seals] and to break its seals?" (**REV.** 5:2).

The answer is given three verses later:

(5) "Behold, the Lion that is from the tribe of Judah, the Root of David, *has overcome* so as to open the book and its seven seals. (6) And I saw between the throne . . . a Lamb standing, *as if slain*" (**REV.** 5:5–6, emphasis added).

Only Jesus Christ, the Lion of Judah, is worthy to open the scroll. When He came the first time, He came as a Lamb to be slaughtered. But His second coming will be vastly different. This time He comes as Judge! It will be the fulfillment of countless prophecies, including the prediction given to the church in the book of Acts:

(30) "God is now declaring to men that all everywhere should repent, (31) because He has fixed a day [the Day of the Lord] in which *He will judge the world* in righteousness through a Man [Christ] whom *He has appointed* [therefore, is worthy], having *furnished proof to all men by raising Him from the dead*" (Acts 17:30–31, emphasis added).

Why is Christ the only One worthy to open the scroll? Because when He came the first time, He overcame the temptation of Sa-

tan, making Christ the perfect Lamb—without spot or blemish—
slain on behalf of His own. As a sign to all that the Father was
pleased with the sacrifice of Christ, the Father raised Him from
the dead and gave Him the right—appointed Him—to judge the
world at the end of the age. Thus, Jesus is the only One worthy to
break the seals, open the scroll and initiate the judgments associated with the Day of the Lord's wrath. By His birth, He became
the legal heir to the Davidic throne. By His death, the Father has
appointed Him to execute His kingly office (Matt. 28:18).

When Christ comes the second time, He will come as the
Lion to destroy the wicked world at the end of the age—during
the Day of the Lord—as in the days of Noah! But first, as promised, He will rescue the righteous before He destroys the
wicked. Then, the kingdom of earth will become the Kingdom
of God over which the Lion of Judah will reign.

*Therefore, if the prewrath position is correct, the thrust of the
Revelation passage we will now look at carefully should show
all three of these critical phases of end time events: the persecution of the elect of God, their deliverance from that persecution,
and the wrath of God upon the wicked world that remains.*

The Supposed Pretribulational Rapture Passage

But first, by way of comparison for what is to follow, let us
look at the single verse that many who hold to the pretribulation view would have us believe is supposedly referring to the
rapture of the saints of God.

> After these things I [John] looked, and behold, a door standing
> open in heaven, and the first voice which I had heard, like the
> sound of a trumpet speaking with me, said, "Come up here, and I
> will show you [John] what must take place after these things"
> (REV. 4:1).

But where is the rapture of the saints described in that
verse? Anyone using the hermeneutic we have agreed upon

must answer, "I don't know. I can't see it!" If you look at the immediate context of this verse, it simply shows a transition from the warnings given to the seven churches on earth concerning the judgment that is to come (chapters 2–3), to the heavenly scene where preparations are being made for this final time of testing and judgment (chapters 4–5), explained in the chapters that follow (chapters 6–19).

Keeping this pretribulational Rapture passage in mind, we will now look carefully at that portion of the book of Revelation that parallels the teaching of Christ in the Olivet Discourse and the teaching of Paul to the church at Thessalonica, taking us to the passage that the prewrath view holds to be the rapture of God's saints, right where it should be, right after the sign of the Day of the Lord is given in the sun, moon, and stars. Then you must be the judge. So let's get started.

The First Seal

After it has been established that Christ, the Lamb of God and the Lion of Judah, is the only One worthy to break the seals and open the scroll, John continues:

(1) And I saw when the Lamb broke one of the seven seals, and I heard one of the four living creatures saying as with a voice of thunder, "Come." (2) And I looked, and behold, a white horse, and he who sat on it had a bow; and a crown was given to him; and he went out conquering, and to conquer (REV. 6:1–2).

When Christ breaks the first seal, one of the four living creatures that surround the throne of Almighty God leaps into action. Obviously, those angelic creatures have been designated to carry out the requirements associated with the breaking of each individual seal before the scroll itself can be opened and the wrath of God can begin. When Scripture is compared with Scripture (in this case, Isa. 6:1–7 with Rev. 4:8), the four living creatures can be identified as God's seraphim. Seraphim are those special angels who surround the throne of God, protecting His holiness by purifying those who come into His presence. The term *seraphim* is derived from a Hebrew word meaning "to burn," which ties directly to their role of purifying. Referring to this same specific period of time, Christ explained to Daniel that during the last days "many will be purged, purified and refined" (Dan. 12:10).

Continuing now with the first seal (Rev. 6:1–2), we see that the rider on the white horse is not identified in the passage itself. Turning to the Olivet Discourse, however, we learn from Christ's own lips that in the last days "many will come in My name, saying, 'I am the Christ,' and will mislead many" (Matt. 24:5). Letting the words of Christ interpret the revelation of Christ, we learn that the first seal represents those whom Christ *permits* to go forth into the world as false Christs. Because the rider is male (he), in the singular form (meaning one), and because "a crown was given to him" (the word "crown" is normally symbolic of rulership, in this instance a position that is specifically given to this particular rider only, going far beyond being just another false Christ), I personally believe this rider to be "the" false Christ of all false Christs, Antichrist!

By now you may be wondering, "What right does Van Kampen have to make such a parallel? Taken at face value, the passage in Revelation makes no reference to the false Christs described by Christ in His Olivet Discourse, to say nothing of making him the Antichrist." That is a good observation and a fair question to ask. In fact, many believe that the rider on the white horse is Christ coming to judge at the Day of the Lord (using Rev. 19:11 as their prooftext), using that interpretation to argue that the wrath of God begins when the first seal is broken. If the first seal were all the evidence we had, I could understand how someone might come to that conclusion. But we must remember that often it is the context that determines meaning. In part, the context of the first seal encompasses the six seals that follow. *It is imperative to keep in mind that the direct author of both accounts is Jesus Christ and that the subject matter of both accounts is the end times.* So, let us look at the six seals that follow, comparing them carefully with the Olivet Discourse. Then you can decide for yourself whether the assumption I am making is a valid one.

The Second Seal

Returning to Revelation 6, we read,

(3) And when He [Christ] broke the second seal, I heard the second living creature saying, "Come." (4) And another, a red horse, went out; and to him who sat on it, it was granted to take peace from the earth, and that men should slay one another; and a great sword was given to him (**REV. 6:3–4**).

Near the beginning of His Olivet Discourse, Christ warned, "For many will come in My name, saying, 'I am the Christ,' and will mislead many" (Matt. 24:5). I took the prerogative of applying that event to the first seal. The next verse goes on to say, "And you will be hearing of wars and rumors of wars; see that you are not frightened, for those things must take place, but that is not yet the end" (Matt. 24:6). That is exactly what happens when the second seal is broken and, with the Lamb's permission, the second horseman begins to unleash his havoc on earth. But, according to Christ's discourse to His disciples, "'that is not yet the end.'" As bad as these first two seals may be, they are not a part of the end of the age—the Day of the Lord. The wrath of God is still to come.

The Third Seal

The parallels referred to earlier become even more apparent when the third seal is broken.

(5) And when He broke the third seal, I heard the third living creature saying, "Come." And I looked, and behold, a black horse; and he who sat on it had a pair of scales in his hand. (6) And I heard as it were a voice in the center of the four living creatures saying, "A quart of wheat for a denarius, and three quarts of barley for a denarius; and do not harm the oil and the wine" (REV. 6:5–6).

The picture that is painted by John is a picture of food shortages that will accompany famine conditions in the world when the third seal is broken. In John's day, a denarius represented a full day's wage, giving us some indication of how highly inflated food prices will be during this time.

Returning to the Olivet Discourse, we see that the next event described by Christ, following the wars and rumors of wars, "will be famines" (Matt. 24:7b). Once again, this perfectly parallels His revelation to John, one account giving the reader an overview of what will occur, the other filling in the details.

Christ then continued to explain to His disciples that "'all these things are merely the beginning of birth pangs'" (Matt. 24:8). In other words, the arrival of the false Christ or Christs (the first seal), the wars and rumors of wars (the second seal), and the famines (the third seal) are nothing compared to what follows next because "'then they will deliver you to tribulation [persecution]. . . . [for] when you see the Abomination of Desolation which was spoken of through Daniel the prophet, standing in the holy place. . . . then there will be a great tribulation, such as has not occurred since the beginning of the world until now, nor ever shall'" (Matt. 24:9, 15, 21).

The Fourth Seal —Satan's Wrath against the Children of God

If we continue to use the Olivet Discourse to interpret Christ's revelation to His bond-servants, we should expect the fourth seal to describe Antichrist's great persecution of the elect of God—the "hard labor," compared to the "beginning birth pangs" of the first three seals. And, sure enough, we see that

> (7) when He broke the fourth seal, I heard the voice of the fourth living creature saying, "Come." (8) And I looked, and behold, an ashen horse; and he who sat on it had the name "Death"; and Hades was following with him. And authority was given to them over a fourth of the earth, to kill with sword and with famine and with pestilence and by the wild beasts of the earth (REV. 6:7–8).

When the fourth seal is broken, the Lamb of God gives Death and Hades the authority to slay a fourth of the earth. Comparing the fourth seal with the Olivet Discourse, we quickly realize that this is the time when the church in general will be put to the true test, separating the genuine bond-servants of Christ from the look-alikes, "on account of My [Christ's] name" (Matt. 24:9)!

A book could be written on Revelation 6:8 alone, but we can only begin to probe its depths here. Because verse 8 deals with the persecution of God's elect at the hands of Antichrist, I have chosen to digress a little and look specifically at what this verse is trying to teach the bond-servants to whom this book is written. We need to look at its different parts to gain a better overview of the thrust of this passage.

Death and Hades

Letting Scripture define Scripture, we find that the term *Death and Hades* is used only three other times in the entire Bible, all three being in the book of Revelation. In two of the three texts (1:18; 20:13), the phrase refers to the temporary abode of the souls of the wicked before they are judged and thrown into the lake of fire at the great white throne judgment of Christ. In the third text (20:14), it can refer to either the temporary abode itself, or it could possibly be a reference to the people who have been kept there, awaiting the judgment of God. Either way, from the context of the fourth seal, when understood in the light of the entire book of Revelation, we know that "Death and Hades" must be a reference to the awful consequences of the wrong choice that many, if not most, men, women, and children will make when the man of lawlessness takes his seat in the temple and demands the worship of the world. We see this borne out by a later passage given in the book of Revelation.

> (9) And another angel, a third one, followed them, saying with a loud voice, "If anyone worships the beast and his image, and receives a mark on his forehead or upon his hand, (10) he also will drink of the wine of the wrath of God, which is mixed in full strength in the cup of His anger; and he will be tormented with fire and brimstone . . ." (Rev. 14:9–10).

In the passage quoted above we see that those who take the mark of Antichrist or worship his image are given a twofold condemnation: *first*, physical death when they face the wrath of God that is still to come; and *then*, Hades, where they will be tormented with fire and brimstone, awaiting the great white throne judgment of Christ when they will be cast forever into the lake of fire. *Death, then Hades, in that order.* "And I looked, and behold, an ashen horse; and he who sat on it had the name 'Death'; and Hades was following with him" (Rev. 6:8).

Authority over a Fourth of the Earth

Again, letting the book of Revelation further explain the fourth seal, we find that

> (2b) the dragon [Satan] gave him [Antichrist] his power and his throne and great authority. . . . (4b) and they [the world] worshiped the beast, saying, "Who is like the beast, and who is able to wage war with him?" . . . (7a) *And it was given to him* [Anti-

christ] *to make war with the saints and to overcome them.* . . . (8) And all who dwell on the earth will worship him, every one whose name has not been written from the foundation of the world in the book of life of the Lamb who has been slain (Rev. 13:2, 4, 7–8, emphasis added).

As the above passage attests, when given the choice, the children of Satan (1 John 3:10) capitulate to Antichrist's demands immediately. It will be the saints who refuse to worship Antichrist—who, if caught, will face "a great tribulation such as has not occurred since the beginning of the world" (Matt. 24:21). But to pursue the saints of God in this manner, first the permission of God must be granted to test the church in general (see 7a above: "*it* [the authority or permission] *was given to him* [Antichrist] to make war with the saints," which parallels Rev. 6:8, "and authority was given to them").

Statistics have been compiled showing the percentage of the world population that belongs to various Judeo-Christian denominations, including the Jewish faith, Protestants, Catholics, Orthodox, and other smaller sects that claim the name of Christ. Together, they comprise almost exactly 25 percent of the world's population. "And authority was given to them *over a fourth of the earth*" (Rev. 6:8, emphasis added).

Why Permit the Church to Be Tested?

The true church has always been promised persecution. "Through many tribulations [same Greek word used in the Olivet Discourse, i.e., Matt. 24:9, 21, 29] we must enter the kingdom of God" (Acts 14:22b). God will permit the church in general to undergo testing by persecution, because the church of the last days will have become severely compromised (2 Thess. 2:3; cf. Matt. 24:9). The testing will reveal who the genuine bond-servants of Christ really are, before the faithful are delivered—rescued—and the wicked are destroyed.

This is further evidenced by the warnings of Christ given to the seven churches in the early chapters of Revelation (2–3), outlining end time consequences for continued compromise and calling on those who have ears to hear—the true bond-servants of Christ—to heed the warnings Christ gives these compromising churches concerning end time events.

Peter put it into the right perspective by explaining

> that the proof of your faith, being more precious than gold which is perishable, *even though tested by fire,* may be found to *result in praise and glory and honor at the revelation of Jesus Christ* (1 Pet. 1:7, emphasis added).

And in his first epistle, John, with the Rapture of the saints in view, exhorts the believer to faithfulness, explaining that the real liar is "the one who denies that Jesus is the Christ"— in other words, the one who chooses Antichrist over Christ (the test—1 John 2:22). Therefore, we should

> abide in Him, so that when He appears, we may have confidence and not shrink away from Him in shame at His coming [*parousía*] (1 John 2:28).

It is for this reason that Christ, like Peter, tells John to refer to this very specific period of time as the

> "hour of *testing [peirasmós],* that hour which is about to come upon the whole world, *to test [peirasmós] those who dwell upon the earth*" (Rev. 3:10, emphasis added; more will be said on this verse in the next chapter).

And this is why Peter, using the same terminology as John, says,

> the Lord knows how to rescue the godly from *temptation [testing—peirasmós],* and to keep the unrighteous under punishment

for the day of judgment [the day of God's wrath] (2 Pet. 2:9, emphasis added).

Thus, Death and Hades must first be given the authority (God's permission) to test and kill, if necessary, those who claim the name of Christ. And, as mentioned earlier, the test will be simple: Whom do you choose to worship, Christ or Antichrist? If they choose Christ, "they will deliver you to tribulation [persecution], and will kill you, and you will be hated by all nations on account of My [Christ's] name" (Matt. 24:9).

Let me finish this thought with some of the saddest verses in the entire Bible:

(10) "And at that time many will fall away [on account of My name] and will deliver up one another and hate one another. . . . [and] (12b) most people's love [for Christ] will grow cold" (Matt. 24:10, 12).

With Sword, with Famine, with Pestilence, by the Beasts

The last phrase of this critical verse (Rev. 6:8) tells the true bond-servant of Christ the methods Satan will use in his attempts to annihilate the saints of God. "By sword, famine, and pestilence (or plague)" is a recurring Old Testament phrase used by the prophets to describe total devastation (see Jer. 14:12; 21:9; 24:10). Thus, the readers or hearers of the book of Revelation would probably have been more familiar with this terminology than we are today. Also, in Ezekiel 14:12–20 wild beasts are referred to alongside sword, famine, and pestilence, although the Greek grammar in our text describing the fourth seal is different. In essence, our text tells us that those who refuse to worship Antichrist will be killed *with* sword, famine, and pestilence *by* (or, to be more precise, *under*) the wild beasts of the earth. The idea in the original language is that the beasts of the earth will be the emissaries through which Death and Hades will directly confront one-fourth of the world's population, having the authority to kill by sword, famine, or pestilence.

Initially, the only really difficult part for me to understand was the meaning of the phrase "by the wild beasts of the earth," and how these beasts of the earth could actually kill by sword, famine, and pestilence, if we wanted to stay true to our face-value hermeneutic.

To kill by sword is clearly a symbolic reference to being hunted down and murdered. The book of Revelation tells us plainly that permission was given Antichrist "to make war with the saints and to overcome them" (Rev. 13:7; cf. 6:8). Famine can also be easily understood in the context of Revelation, in light of the fact that those without the mark can neither buy nor sell (Rev. 13:16–17), even at the highly inflated prices indicated when the third seal is broken. Unless prepared in advance, you can't buy food, even if you can afford it. And if you can't buy food, you don't eat. And if you don't eat, you die. Just that simple. Likewise, the concept of killing by pestilence or plague is not that hard to understand, although I have not yet found the passage in Revelation that describes how this is actually accomplished.[1]

But my real question persisted, still unanswered. Why do the Scriptures tell us that these things will be brought about *under* the direction of or *by* means of the wild beasts?[2] How could they be the emissaries of Death and Hades to destroy the saints of God who refuse to worship Antichrist?

1. The Greek word used by John in Rev. 6:8 for pestilence or plague, *thánatos*, actually is translated *death* in the English (as in Death [*thánatos*] and Hades). But this is the same Greek word that the Septuagint (LXX—which was the Greek translation of the Hebrew Bible written in the third century B.C., primarily used by the first-century church) used when translating the Hebrew word for plague or pestilence into the Greek. Because of the parallel to similar events in Jeremiah and Ezekiel, and because of how the LXX sometimes translated *thánatos*, it is translated *pestilence*, not *death*, the second time it is used in our text (Rev. 6:8).

2. *Hupo*, translated "under" or "by," is usually used to refer to people when used in this grammatical construction.

My answer came when I realized that it had been obscured because of a poor English translation. The Greek word *thē-rión*, here translated "wild beasts," is used thirty-eight times in the book of Revelation. Except in this one instance referred to when the fourth seal is broken, the Greek word is translated "beast," and is a direct reference either to Antichrist himself (13:3–4)—"it was given to him to make war with the saints" (13:7), the second beast who assists Antichrist—"he exercises all the authority of the first beast [to make war with the saints]" (13:12), or to the enlivened image of the beast who will cause those who "do not worship the image of the beast to be killed" (13:15).

There was my answer, plain and simple. Death, and Hades who follows close behind, will be given authority over a quarter of the earth's population—over those who profess the name of Christ. The emissaries of Death and Hades will be the beasts of Revelation: Antichrist (the beast), his enforcer (the second beast), and the enlivened image of the beast. The test will be simple. Whom will you worship, Christ or Antichrist? Those who choose Christ over Antichrist will die by means of sword, famine, and plague (Matt. 24:9; cf. Rev. 13:7, 10, 15). Those who reject the name of Christ (Matt. 24:9–10) for the sake of Antichrist (Rev. 13:8) "will drink of the wine of the wrath of God . . . and he will be tormented with fire and brimstone in the presence of the holy angels and in the presence of the Lamb" (Rev. 14:10). Death, then Hades. The choice every man, woman, and child who professes the name of Christ will have to make when confronted by the beasts of Revelation.

In this context, a passage we have already looked at takes on even more meaning:

(22) Who is the liar but the one who denies that Jesus is the Christ? This is the antichrist, the one who denies the Father and the Son. . . . (28) And now, little children, abide in Him, so that

when He appears, we may have confidence and not shrink away
from Him in shame at His coming (1 John 2:22, 28).

The Fifth Seal

Moving on now to the fifth seal, we see the tragic results of
the test given to the whole world:

(9) And when He [Christ] broke the fifth seal, I saw underneath
the altar the souls of those who had been slain because of the word
of God, and because of the testimony which they had maintained;
(10) and they cried out with a loud voice, saying, *"How long, O
Lord, holy and true, wilt Thou refrain from judging and avenging
our blood on those who dwell on the earth?"* (11) *And there was
given to each of them a white robe; and they were told that they
should rest for a little while longer, until the number of their fellow
servants and their brethren who were to be killed even as they had
been, should be completed also* (**REV. 6:9–11**, emphasis added).

The fifth seal reflects the death toll caused by Antichrist's
persecution. In the Olivet Discourse, Christ says that when
"they will deliver you to tribulation [the fourth seal]," they "will
kill you . . . on account of My name" [the fifth seal] (Matt. 24:9).
The fourth seal gives Satan the authority—the permission necessary—to test the whole world, in particular, the professing
church that represents 25 percent of the world's population; the
fifth seal shows that some will die for their allegiance to the true
Christ, again paralleling precisely the sequence of events that
Christ gave His disciples in the Olivet Discourse.

Two items of interest in this fifth seal passage should be
noted.

First, notice that the martyrs are asking God, "How long, O
Lord, holy and true, wilt Thou refrain from judging and avenging our blood on those who dwell on the earth?" (Rev. 6:10).
Those martyred saints know full well that their martyrdom was
not at the hands of God (i.e., the wrath of God), as their testi-

mony attests. What they want to know is *when* God will retaliate with His divine wrath against those who have put them to death—the very message contained in Paul's second letter to the Thessalonians:

> (6) For after all *it is only just for God to repay with affliction those who afflict you,* (7) and to give relief to you who are afflicted and to us as well when the Lord Jesus shall be revealed from heaven with His mighty angels in flaming fire, (8) *dealing out retribution to those who do not know God* . . . (2 Thess. 1:6–8, emphasis added).

The second interesting point about this fifth-seal passage concerns the answer that is given to the martyrs' question. They are told to wait "until the number of their fellow servants and their brethren who were to be killed even as they had been, should be completed also" (Rev. 6:11).

The Olivet Discourse teaches that God will "cut short" the days of Antichrist's persecution (see Matt. 24:21–22) when the sign is given in the sun, moon, and stars (vv. 29–31), and the fifth seal gives us the condition that will trigger these end time events. God knows the number of men and women who will die for Christ instead of capitulating to Antichrist. When that number is complete, then, and not a moment earlier, God will give His sign in the heavens—in the sun, moon, and stars—and then the *parousía* of Christ will be seen in the heavenlies. Then Christ will rescue every righteous person who "endures to the end" (Matt. 24:13). "And then the end shall come" (Matt. 24:14), at which time the Lord will unleash His wrath against the wicked who remain.

The Sixth Seal —Sign of the Day of the Lord

If we continue to use the Olivet Discourse as the yardstick by which we measure the book of Revelation, we know that when the number of martyrs is complete (which, by definition, must mean that the persecution by Antichrist has been brought to an end), the very next event that must occur (if the book of Revelation indeed parallels the Olivet Discourse) will be the all-important sign of the Day of the Lord. If that is indeed the case, the next seal should be the promised sign that will be given in the sun, moon, and stars announcing to the world that the great day of God's wrath is about to occur!

> (12) And I looked when He broke the sixth seal, and there was a great earthquake; and the sun became black as sackcloth made of hair, and the whole moon became like blood; (13) and the stars of the sky fell to the earth, as a fig tree casts its unripe figs when shaken by a great wind. (14) And the sky was split apart like a scroll when it is rolled up; and every mountain and island were moved out of their places. (15) And the kings of the earth and the great men and the commanders and the rich and the strong and every slave and free man, hid themselves in the caves and among the rocks of the mountains; (16) and they said to the mountains and to the rocks, "Fall on us and hide us from the presence of Him who sits on the throne, and from the wrath of the Lamb; (17) for the great day of their wrath has come; and who is able to stand?" (REV. 6:12–17, emphasis added).

What could be added to so descriptive a passage? If you have understood the sequences argued in the previous chapters of this book, this passage should be self-explanatory. *After* the "hard labor" begins (the great persecution by Antichrist, the fourth seal), and *after* a specific number of faithful men and women have been martyred for the sake of Christ's name (the fifth seal), *then* the sign of the Day of the Lord will be given in the heavens (the sixth seal)! When this occurs, the followers of Antichrist will say, "Hide us from the presence of Him who sits on the throne, and from the wrath of the Lamb; *for the great day of their wrath has come; and who is able to stand?*" (Rev. 6:16–17; cf. Isa. 2:19, 21, emphasis added).

Plain and simple, right? The sign given in the sun, moon, and stars is the sign of the Day of the Lord, the precursor to the initiation of God's wrath. It may be clear to us, but those who want the Rapture to occur *before* the seven-year tribulation period begins, must make the wrath of God—referred to when the sixth seal is broken—begin back when the first seal was broken. Therefore, they will argue that the statement, "the great day of their wrath has come," does not mean *the great day of their wrath has come,* but rather, *the great day of their wrath began way back when the first seal was opened!*

The Attack

The critical phrase in this key passage is the phrase "has come," which is a translation of the Greek verb *elthein. Elthein* is in the aorist tense, indicative mood of *érchomai,* the most common Greek verb for "come." Those holding to the pretribulation position will tell you that because *elthein* is in the aorist tense, it must therefore refer to an action that began sometime in the past and has already been going on for some time, right up to the present. They will tell you that any verb in the aorist tense *always* refers to an action that began sometime in the past.

The Defense

For the sake of brevity, I will just touch upon why this rigid position on the aorist tense leads to a misunderstanding of the sequence of events in Revelation. The aorist tense is, generally speaking, timeless. In narration, it can be used to describe the simple past. Another common use of the aorist tense is to describe the beginning of something. This is called the ingressive use of the aorist, and is clearly the use in this context.

Because the word *wrath* is not mentioned in the book of Revelation prior to the sixth seal, and because the signs given in the sun, moon, and stars referred to in the sixth seal parallel the signs that will occur announcing the day of the Lord's wrath (Joel 2:31; cf. Matt. 24:29–31, 37–39), the context of our present text seems self-evident. It is an event that is on the threshold of happening—a future event soon to occur.

By way of comparison, we find the use of the identical Greek word, *elthein*, by Christ in the Garden of Gethsemane. The context here, like the context of our text in Revelation, is an excellent example of the ingressive use of the aorist, describing an event just about to occur.

> (41) And He came the third time, and said to them, "Are you still sleeping and taking your rest? It is enough; the hour has come [*elthein*]; behold, the Son of Man is being betrayed into the hands of sinners. (42) Arise, let us be going; behold, the one who betrays Me is at hand!" (43) And immediately while He was speaking, Judas . . . (Mark 14:41–43).

Enough said. Whether the word refers to past action or action just on the verge of occurring is obvious from the context—as it is in the sixth-seal passage!

And if the context were not clear, by simply comparing the sixth seal with the Olivet Discourse, any question as to when the sixth-seal events begin would be immediately clarified by the very words of Christ. That's called comparing Scripture with Scripture!

Now, after the sign given in the sun, moon, and stars announces to the world what is to follow, the Olivet Discourse tells us that

> (30) then the sign of the Son of Man will appear in the sky, and then all the tribes of the earth will mourn, and they will see the Son of Man coming on the clouds of the sky with power and great glory. (31) And *He will send forth His angels with a great trumpet and they will gather together His elect from the four winds, from one end of the sky to the other* (Matt. 24:30–31, emphasis added).

First the sign, then the Rapture—which, by definition, brings Antichrist's persecution of God's elect to an abrupt end! You can't persecute something that has been removed from your grasp! That being the case, what must now follow in the book of Revelation is a description of the rapture of God's faithful. And that is exactly what happens. Not just an isolated verse in chapter 4, as those holding to the pretribulation Rapture view would have you believe, but an extensive passage taking the better part of an entire chapter. Judge for yourselves!

The Rapture

The seventh chapter of Revelation immediately follows the breaking of the sixth seal, and the two events recorded in this chapter occur *simultaneously*. As we mentioned earlier, the book of Revelation tracks both the promises to Israel given in the Old Testament and the promises to the church given in the New Testament. Because the first of the two events recorded here deals directly with promises given to Israel, the Jewish portion of chapter 7 has little relevance to the sequence of events surrounding the rapture of the genuine bond-servants of Christ. However, for those of you who might be wondering, this first portion of the chapter describes God's sealing of 144,000 Jews for protection against the wrath of God that is soon to follow (see Rev. 9:4). We referred to this briefly back in chapter 3, in the point that dealt with the wrath of God. These 144,000 will become the firstfruits of unsaved Israel (Rev. 14:4), not saved until the Rapture occurs—which is why they will not be raptured with the saints—and soon to become the inhabitants of the Millennial Kingdom on earth over which Christ will rule.

It is the other event described in this chapter that directly concerns the elect of God who will have been undergoing Antichrist's persecution, those who have been promised deliverance because of their faithfulness to Christ during this great time of Satanic testing. After the sign is given in the sun, moon, and stars, then

(9) I looked, and behold, a great multitude, which no one could count, from every nation and all tribes and peoples and tongues, standing before the throne and before the Lamb, clothed in white robes, and palm branches were in their hands; (10) and they cry out with a loud voice, saying, "Salvation [deliverance] to our God who sits on the throne, and to the Lamb." (11) And all the angels were standing around the throne and around the elders and the four living creatures; and they fell on their faces before the throne and worshiped God, (12) saying, "Amen, blessing and glory and wisdom and thanksgiving and honor and power and might, be to our God forever and ever" (**REV. 7:9–12**, emphasis added).

Identification of the Great Multitude

Who is this great multitude that suddenly appears before the throne of God (vv. 9, 11)? After comparing Scripture to Scripture, I can't see how this great multitude can be anyone other than the raptured saints of God, along with those resurrected who had previously died "in Jesus." Paul, in his first letter to the Thessalonians, asked that Christ would

establish your hearts unblamable in holiness before our God and Father at the coming of our Lord Jesus with all His saints (1 Thess. 3:13).

Clearly, Paul is referring to what John is now seeing firsthand in heaven—the arrival of the great multitude before the throne of God the Father in heaven.

But there are other very good reasons why this text must refer to the arrival of the saints, dead and living, before the throne of Almighty God. Follow my reasoning carefully and see if you don't agree.

First, the timing of the arrival of this great multitude in heaven *precisely parallels* the timing Christ gave His disciples in the Olivet Discourse, as to when the elect of God would be gathered together—raptured—from one end of the sky to the other (Matt. 24:29, 31), an event that occurs immediately following the announcement of God's wrath in the sun, moon, and stars. *If every other detail associated with the seals of Revelation has so perfectly paralleled the Olivet Discourse thus far, should not the Olivet Discourse provide the identification of this great multitude as well?*

Second, this "great multitude which no one could count" is described by John as coming "from every nation and all tribes and peoples and tongues." Comparing Scripture with Scripture, we see that this great multitude is described with the same terminology that the heavenly beings used in describing those for whom Christ died, "from every tribe and tongue and people and nation" (5:9), two chapters earlier in Revelation. If this specific but unusual terminology is used in chapter 5 to describe the elect of God from the beginning of time, those for whom Christ died, why wouldn't the identical terminology be a reference to the same group of men and women when it is used again just two chapters later?

Next, this great multitude is praising God for their deliverance. The Greek phrase translated "salvation to our God" is more accurately translated, "let salvation [or, even better, deliverance] be ascribed to our God." Are those saints praising God for their spiritual salvation or for their physical deliverance from the persecution occurring on earth? Remember, Christ taught His disciples that "the one who endures to the end, he shall be saved [delivered]" (Matt. 24:13), using the same Greek root word (saved, delivered) used in the Revelation passage (salvation, deliverance). There is no way to be sure, but I would guess that this great multitude that suddenly arrives in heaven will be praising Him for both those blessings.

In addition, it is interesting to note that when this great multitude first arrives in heaven, they are greeted by the Father (v. 11), the Lamb (v. 9), all the angels (v. 11), the twenty-four elders (v. 11), and the four living creatures (v. 11), but no mention is made of the raptured or resurrected elect of God from ages past! If this great multitude is a reference to someone other than the raptured and resurrected saints of God, then you must ask yourself, where are they, if indeed the Rapture occurred back in Revelation 4:1? Could it possibly be that this great multitude includes the raptured bond-servants of Christ, especially in light of the fact that the timing here in Revelation perfectly parallels the timing of the Rapture given us by Christ and by Paul?

But I have kept the best argument for last. Notice that when this great multitude arrives in heaven, they are seen "standing before the throne . . . clothed in white robes . . . palm branches in their hands" (v. 9).

You may wonder, "So what?" to which I respond, "They have bodies, and the elect will not receive resurrected bodies until the Rapture!" Even the fifth-seal martyrs don't receive their resurrected bodies until the first day of the millennium (Rev. 20:4). So if these new arrivals have bodies, they have to be those who have been raptured or resurrected at the coming of the Lord, "caught up together . . . to meet the Lord in the air" (1 Thess. 4:17).

Paul exults in his first letter to the church at Corinth,

> (51) Behold, I tell you a mystery; we shall not all sleep, but we shall all be changed, (52) in a moment, in the twinkling of an eye, at the last trumpet; for the trumpet will sound, *and the dead will be raised imperishable, and we shall be changed* (1 Cor. 15:51–52, emphasis added).

Every genuine believer receives his or her resurrection body at the second coming of Christ and not a moment before. This great multitude that suddenly arrive in heaven have bodies. Two plus two always equals four; thus, a great multitude suddenly arriving in heaven with bodies can only be the raptured saints who are taken up into heaven along with the resurrected "dead in Christ"! And finally, the frosting on the cake!

(13) And one of the elders answered, saying to me, "These who are clothed in the white robes, who are they, and from where have they come?" (14) And I said to him, "My lord, you know." And he said to me, *"These are the ones who come out of the great tribulation* [persecution], and they have washed their robes and made them white in the blood of the Lamb" (**REV. 7:13–14**, emphasis added).

If any doubt still lingers in your mind as to the identity of this great multitude and where they will come from, this last passage should remove it. For it clearly shows that "these are the ones who come out of the great tribulation," *directly identifying this great multitude as the elect of God that Christ refers to in the Olivet Discourse, who will be gathered together from the four winds when the great tribulation by Antichrist is cut short by the signs given in the sun, moon, and stars.*

It is interesting to note that the Greek preposition *ek*, here translated "out of," more precisely means "to come out from the midst of," which accurately describes what happens to the saints of God when Antichrist's persecution is cut short by the events associated with the coming (*parousía*) of the Son of Man.

Again, the Attack

But once again, as with the Greek verb *eltheín* in its relationship to the sixth seal, those who hold to the pretribulation Rapture position will try to tell you that this great multitude "who *come* out of the great tribulation" should be translated as the great multitude "who *are coming* out of the great tribulation." They will tell you that the Greek word *erchómenoi*, translated "come," is a present participle that is often translated "coming." Obviously, if this great multitude can be shown as arriving over a period of time, their identification as the raptured ones suddenly arriving in heaven after Antichrist's persecution is abruptly "cut short" becomes a little more difficult to explain. On the other hand, if this great multitude arrives all at the same time, their identification as the raptured saints of the church is greatly enhanced, paralleling precisely the Olivet Discourse.

And Again, the Defense

The apparent problem at this point is caused by not understanding simple principles of grammar. The "time" of a Greek sentence is fixed by the verb of the sentence in its context, not by a participle. Thus, in this case the participial phrase, "the ones who are coming out of the great tribulation," is attached to a sequence of two Greek verbs in the aorist tense. The two aorist verbs to which this participle has been attached are translated "have washed" and "made," both in the past tense, both referring to an event that has already been completed before the eyes of the onlookers. The point is that it is these verbs that tell us the timing of the event being described, not the participle. In this case, the present participle is being used to vividly describe a past event, something that has just happened.

This is also why one of the elders refers to this great multitude as having already arrived. "'These who are clothed in the white robes, who are they, and from where have they *come* [*elthon*]?'"—the verb *elthon* being the past tense of the Greek verb "to come." Certainly if the elder had been witnessing an ever-increasing multitude, getting larger as he watched, the past tense of the verb "to come" would not have been the appropriate tense to use. Rather, he would have asked, "Who are they and from where are they *coming*?" But that is not how the question is posed. The great multitude in its entirety had just arrived, "'and they have *washed* [past tense] their robes and *made* [past tense] them white in the blood of the Lamb.'"

Thus, by comparing Scripture with Scripture and applying a little common sense, we see that this great multitude must describe the raptured saints and the resurrected "dead in Christ," now "standing" before the throne of God. Thus, the sixth seal represents the sign of the Day of the Lord—"the sun became black as sackcloth . . . the whole moon became like blood . . . the stars of the sky fell to the earth . . . for the great day of their wrath has come" (Rev. 6:12–17)—and the seventh chapter of Revelation shows the deliverance, or rapture, of God's faithful, "'the ones who come out of the great tribulation'" (Rev. 7:14). And then, the wrath of God . . .

The Seventh Seal —God's Wrath against the Children of Satan

If we continue to follow the parallel sequence outlined in the Olivet Discourse of Christ, as well as the imagery associated with the breaking of the seven seals—opening the scroll and initiating the wrath of God—when the seventh and last seal on the scroll is finally broken, we should expect the wrath of God to begin against the wicked who remain on earth. And that is exactly what we find. For

(1) when He broke the seventh seal, there was silence in heaven for about half an hour. (2) And I saw the seven angels who stand before God; and seven trumpets were given to them. (3) And another angel came and stood at the altar, holding a golden censer. . . . (5) . . . and he filled it with the fire of the altar and threw it to the earth; and there followed peals of thunder and sounds and flashes of lightning and an earthquake. (6) And the seven angels who had the seven trumpets prepared themselves to sound them (REV. 8:1–3, 5–6).

With the breaking of the seventh seal, the scroll is finally loosed and the day of God's *fiery* judgment begins. First, anticipating the fiery wrath of God that is about to begin, there will be silence in heaven for half an hour. Then, taking a golden censer, an angel "filled it with the fire of the altar [from where the martyrs have just asked, "How long, O Lord . . . ?"] and threw it to the earth."

Peter tells us that in Noah's day, God destroyed the earth the first time by water (2 Pet. 3:6). The rainbow was God's promise never to destroy the world again in this manner (Gen. 9:11–13). But, Peter says, "the present heavens and earth by His word are being reserved for fire, kept for the day of judgment and destruction of ungodly men" (2 Pet. 3:7). The last time God will destroy the entire earth, during the Day of the Lord, He will destroy it by fire, giving the scene in heaven even more significance.

After the angel fills his golden censer with fire from the altar and throws the fire down to the earth, the seven angels begin to sound their fiery trumpet judgments upon the earth:

> And the first [trumpet] sounded, and there came hail and *fire* mixed with blood, and they were thrown to the earth; and *a third of the earth was burned up* . . . (**REV. 8:7**, emphasis added).

When the first trumpet sounds, the day of God's great wrath will finally begin, *precisely following* the overview given by Christ to His disciples in His Olivet Discourse, as well as the sequence of events Paul had given to the church of Thessalonica.

Summing It Up

There you have it. I realize that this has not been an in-depth study, but it has been consistent, using the same hermeneutic from beginning to end, comparing Scripture with Scripture, letting the Word of God interpret itself. When the teaching of Christ in the Olivet Discourse is compared with the writings of Paul and John concerning end times—and in particular, the timing of when the true saints of God will be raptured—the same sequence is given, over and over again. First the persecution by Antichrist against the elect of God (Satan's wrath), then God's deliverance of the faithful (the Rapture), followed by the Day of the Lord (God's wrath upon those who remain). Plain and simple.

In summary, then, let us review the sequence of events outlined by Christ to John in the book of Revelation, with the parallel teaching Christ gave His disciples in the Olivet Discourse.

Both accounts are given in the context of Christ's specific warning that what is revealed in those passages must be taken seriously by His followers (Matt. 24:4; cf. Rev. 22:19).

Both accounts begin their descriptions of the last days with a reference to false Christs—*the first seal* (Matt. 24:5; cf. Rev. 6:1–2).

Both accounts warn of wars and rumors of wars—*the second seal* (Matt. 24:6–7; cf. Rev. 6:3–4).

Both accounts warn of a great time of famine—*the third seal* (Matt. 24:7; cf. Rev. 6:5–6).

Both accounts warn of a time of intense persecution of God's elect—*the fourth seal* (Matt. 24:9, 21; cf. Rev. 6:7–8).

Both accounts make reference to the martyrdom of the elect, God's saints—*the fifth seal* (Matt. 24:9, 22; cf. Rev. 6:9).

Both accounts show that Antichrist's persecution will be limited—*the fifth seal* (Matt. 24:22; cf. Rev. 6:11).

Both accounts show that sometime during Antichrist's persecution of God's elect, a sign will be given in the sun, moon, and stars, announcing the Day of the Lord's wrath—*the sixth seal* (Matt. 24:29; cf. Rev. 6:12–17).

Both accounts show the rapture—deliverance—of God's elect from out of the midst of the "great tribulation," abruptly terminating Antichrist's persecution of God's elect just before the wrath of God begins—*the interlude between the sixth and seventh seals* (Matt. 24:29–31; cf. Rev. 7:9–14).

Both accounts show the commencement of God's wrath, the Day of the Lord—*the seventh seal* (Matt. 24:37–39; cf. Rev. 8:1–7).

Thus, the major events described in the Olivet Discourse parallel the major events described in the book of Revelation,

COMPARATIVE ACCOUNTS

The Olivet Discourse (Matt. 24) and the Book of Revelation (Chpts. 6-8)

The Olivet Discourse of Christ		The Revelation of Christ	
24:4	**WARNING** To God's Elect	22:19	**WARNING**
24:5	**FALSE CHRISTS**	6:1-2	**THE FIRST SEAL**
24:6	**WARS**	6:3-4	**THE SECOND SEAL**
24:7	**FAMINES**	6:5-6	**THE THIRD SEAL**
24:9,21	**THE GREAT TRIBULATION**	6:7-8	**THE FOURTH SEAL**
24:9,22	Death	6:9	**THE FIFTH SEAL**
24:10,24	Apostasy		
24:29	**SIGN OF THE END OF THE AGE** Sun, Moon and Stars	6:12-17	**THE SIXTH SEAL**
24:30,27	**SIGN OF CHRIST'S COMING**		
24:30	**THE COMING OF CHRIST**		
24:13,31	**THE DELIVERANCE OF CHRIST'S ELECT** The Rapture	7:9-14	**THE GREAT MULTITUDE** Out of the Great Tribulation
24:14, 37-39	**THE WRATH OF GOD** The End of the Age or The Day of the Lord	8:1-7	**THE SEVENTH SEAL**

right up to and including the breaking of the seventh seal when the wrath of God begins.

At the precise point that the Olivet Discourse shows the elect of God being gathered from the four winds by the angels of Christ, when the great tribulation associated with Antichrist is cut short, the book of Revelation shows a great multitude, without number, coming out from the midst of the great tribulation by Antichrist and suddenly arriving in heaven, before the throne of God, with their resurrection bodies. Are these parallel passages describing the Rapture or the battle of Armageddon? Well, the arrival of the great multitude is in chapter 7 of Revelation. The battle of Armageddon doesn't even occur until much later in the sequence of end time events, not until chapter 19.

Rapture or Armageddon? You must decide. And remember, your decision will directly affect how you prepare for the last days, when

"[they] will kill you, and you will be hated by all nations on account of My name. . . . for then there will be a great tribulation, such as has not occurred since the beginning of the world until now, nor ever shall" (Matt. 24:9, 21).

8

That's Greek to Me

This chapter will deal with what has been for me the last important piece to the puzzle, reinforcing all that we have worked through together in the previous chapters. Through my own study, I have learned that a proper understanding of the original languages of Scripture always adds light and clarity to God's message, and it has been exciting for me to discover and understand the meanings of certain Greek words found in some of the critical passages that deal with the end times. Each time, the original Greek text has just reconfirmed the prewrath position. (We have seen numerous examples of this already in several chapters of this book.)

I realize that this is a bold statement to make, so instead of simply taking my word for it, I want you to follow my reasoning and, once again, decide for yourself.

Some of you may think this Greek word study will be over your head. I can assure you, it will be anything but that. You will understand what is said, even if you forget the Greek! It will greatly enhance your own understanding of God's Word, so hang in there with me just a little longer.

When really grappling with what a certain text means, I constantly remind myself that the study of God's Word is a holy calling. It is not for the lazy, the faint of heart, the stubborn, or the proud. It is hard work, and it must be pursued as an offering of gratitude and unblemished love. Like the high priest of Old Testament times, we must take care when entering this holy place. We should approach our study of God's Word by the work of Christ and the grace of God.

The Revelation 3:10 Controversy

To begin with, then, I would like to carefully look at the one passage that pretribulationists will most often use in their attempt to keep the church out of the great persecution by Antichrist. In fairness, some of them who know their Greek will admit that this passage, in the original language, does not make the argument that the English translation seems to make. But most will adamantly point to this single verse to support their pretribulation view, thinking it to be their best hope of defending their position—and it is an especially good argument if the person they are trying to convince has no knowledge of the Greek grammar that underlies this particular passage. *In reality, however, we shall see that the underlying Greek text proves the prewrath position, not the pretrib position, so follow with me carefully.*

First, let's look at the English translation of this passage before examining the Greek text from which this passage has been translated.

> (7) "And to the angel of the church in Philadelphia write. . . . (10) 'Because you have kept the word of My perseverance, *I also will keep you from the hour of testing, that hour which is about to come upon the whole world,* to test those who dwell upon the earth'" (Rev. 3:7, 10, emphasis added).

Those who hold to the pretribulation Rapture view will point to this passage, which appears to say that God "will keep" the faithful *"from* the hour of testing." Because there is little dispute in most evangelical circles concerning the fact that the hour of testing referred to in our text is a reference to all or part of the final seven-year tribulation period, including, but not limited to, Antichrist's time of intense persecution, you can understand why those holding to the pretrib view might be tempted to use this passage to prove their argument that the church will be raptured away from earth before the seven-year tribulation period ever begins. But is that really what the passage is teaching? To know precisely, we must go to the original language.

There are three key phrases in this verse, and we must look at the Greek text underlying each of these before we can fully understand what this verse is saying. We will look at them in the following order: "Because you have kept the word of My perseverance, I also will keep you"; "the hour of testing"; and then the really critical phrase, "keep you from."

The Word of Thy Perseverance

The Greek behind the rendering of this somewhat awkward phrase, "because you have kept the word of My perseverance, I also will keep you," is crystal clear. First, there is a wordplay on the verb "to keep," as the identical Greek verb (*tēréō*) is used twice in this verse. The primary meaning of *tēréō* is "to guard, watch over, or keep." It is also commonly used in the New Testament to mean "to observe or follow." The idea being conveyed in this verse is *a cause-and-effect type of relationship:* because you have *kept* . . . I also will *keep.* . . . "Because you have observed or followed something of great value to Me, therefore, I will guard or watch over something of great value to you" is the idea the writer is conveying by the double use of the verb *tēréō.*

The first question we should ask, then, is this: What have we kept—followed or observed, as it were—that has such value to Christ that obligates Him to give us something in return? The answer is, "The word of My [Christ's] perseverance." That is such an awkward phrase because of the way it has been translated. A better translation would be, "because you have followed or observed My instruction to you concerning perseverance, I will. . . ." Or, better yet, Christ "will keep you" because you "have kept"—observed or followed—His instruction concerning perseverance (i.e., because you have been faithful to Me, I will be faithful to you).

And so, logically, the next question we should be asking ourselves is this: "What instruction concerning perseverance have the faithful been following that so delights the heart of our Lord in this end time context?" It is the context of the verse that gives us our answer: the faithful have observed or followed Christ's instruction concerning "perseverance." Notice that in Revelation 3:8 we are told that this faithful church of Philadelphia had "kept My word and have not denied My name." Thus, as it was in the days that John instructed the church of Philadelphia, so likewise in the last days the church will once again be called upon to persevere for the sake of Christ's name.

Christ's teaching on the subject of perseverance in the last days can be found in three separate passages. The first is in our overview text of end times that Christ gave His disciples in the Olivet Discourse:

(9) *"Then they will deliver you to tribulation,* and will kill you, and you will be hated by all nations on account of My name. . . . (13) *But the one who endures to the end,* he shall be *saved [delivered]"* (Matt. 24:9, 13, emphasis added).

The one who *endures* to the end will be *delivered!* Endures what? Endures the persecution associated with the rule of Antichrist (v. 9). Another cause-and-effect promise, similar to the cause-and-effect promise recorded in Revelation 3:10. Interestingly, "endured" (Matt. 24:9) or "persevered" (Rev. 3:10), are two different forms of the same Greek word, found in two separate passages, and both originating from Christ.

And if enduring or persevering through Antichrist's persecution is "the word of My [Christ's] perseverance" to which our passage in Revelation refers, this instruction, given to a church to begin with (see Rev. 3:7), would rightfully contradict those using Revelation 3:10 as a prooftext for the pretribulation Rapture position, which removes the church before this time of tribulation ever occurs. Before we come to that conclusion, however, we need to look at the two other passages that contain the instruction of Christ concerning the last days—the instruction Christ gave to John in Revelation.

In these two passages, the who, what, and when of this time of perseverance are very specific. It is again important to note that these two passages are the only instances in which this key Greek word—translated *perseverance*—is used in the entire book of Revelation outside the general warning given to the churches in chapters 2 and 3.

(7) And it was given to him [Antichrist] to make war with the *saints* and to overcome them. . . . (10) If anyone is destined for captivity, to captivity he goes; if anyone kills with the sword, with the sword he must be killed. Here is the *perseverance and the faith of the saints* (Rev. 13:7, 10, emphasis added).

(9) And another angel, a third one, followed them, saying with a loud voice, "*If anyone worships the beast [Antichrist] and his image, and receives a mark on his forehead or upon his hand,* (10) he also will drink of the wine of the wrath of God, which is mixed in full strength in the cup of His anger; and he will be tormented with fire and brimstone in the presence of the holy angels and in the presence of the Lamb." . . . (12) *Here is the perseverance of the*

saints who keep the commandments of God and their faith in Jesus
(Rev. 14:9–10, 12, emphasis added).

In both of these passages the word of Christ's perseverance
(3:10) is directly associated with the "perseverance of the
saints" (13:10 and 14:12) during the persecution at the hands
of Antichrist (13:7 and 14:9)! Like the instruction of Christ to
His disciples, these two passages again identify the saints as
those who refuse to worship the Antichrist, who choose, rather,
to keep the "faith" or "keep the commandments of God." In
other words, those who choose to "keep the commandments of
God" is just another way of referring to those who choose to
"observe or follow My instruction concerning perseverance,"
rather than cave in to the demands of Antichrist!

So the first phrase is very meaningful in our understanding
of Revelation 3:10. Clearly the teaching of Christ concerning
perseverance in the last days is to the elect or saints of God
who persevere during Antichrist's time of persecution, rather
than yield to his demands!

The Hour of Whose Testing?

Next, we need to look very carefully at the second phrase,
"the hour of testing." Those who hold to the pretribulation
Rapture view agree that this "hour of testing" is either the entire seven-year tribulation period or, at a minimum, the time of
Antichrist's persecution of God's elect (the second half of the
tribulation period), in part because the very next verse directly
refers to the second coming of Christ. "I am coming quickly;
hold fast what you have, in order that no one take your crown"
(v. 11). They would also agree, across the board, that the "hour
of testing" is the wrath of God during the Day of the Lord, from
which the church is exempted. But is this time of testing the
wrath of God, or is this time of testing the wrath of Satan?

Once again, when the underlying Greek text is studied carefully, comparing Scripture with Scripture, we will discover

that the "hour of testing" refers specifically to that time associated with Antichrist's persecution, in the same manner in which Christ's instruction concerning perseverance concerns *our* perseverance *during* Antichrist's persecution. *More important, we will see that the Greek words underlying our English translations argue that this terrible time of testing cannot be the wrath of God, but must be the wrath of Satan.*

The Greek word translated "testing" is *peirasmós*, which means "a putting to the proof," either for good or for evil. Now let's look at this specific term translated "testing," logically and then biblically. Logically, why do we need to put something to the proof *after* the Rapture has already separated the righteous from the wicked? It seems to me that you should put something to the proof *before* you make a decision about its value. Then, based on the outcome of that testing, you take the appropriate steps and make the necessary distinctions or separations.

The biblical argument is even more convincing. If the Greek word *peirasmós*, as used in the Revelation 3:10 passage, is compared to its use in other New Testament passages, we will see that the "hour of testing" cannot refer to the wrath of God but, quite the opposite, to the wrath of Satan. For example, James warns,

> Let no one say when he is *tempted*, "I am being tempted by God"; for God cannot be *tempted* by evil, and *He Himself does not tempt any one* (James 1:13, emphasis added).

The Greek word that James uses here for the verb "tempted," *peirazó*, comes from the same root, *peira*, as does the noun *peirasmós*, translated "testing" in Revelation 3:10. Therefore, if God does not tempt (*peirazó*) anyone to do evil, how can the "hour of testing" (*peirasmós*) be the wrath of God?

But, you may argue, even if *peirasmós* or *peirazó* is not of God, how can it be proved that the "testing" (*peirasmós*) referred to in these verses originates from Satan? Look now at the three following passages, which I think speak for themselves:

> For this reason, when I could endure it no longer, I also sent to find out about your faith, for fear that the *tempter* might have *tempted* you, and our labor should be in vain (1 Thess. 3:5, emphasis added).

> Stop depriving one another, except by agreement for a time that you may devote yourselves to prayer, and come together again lest *Satan tempt you* because of your lack of self-control (1 Cor. 7:5, emphasis added).

> Then Jesus was led up by the Spirit into the wilderness to be *tempted by the devil* (Matt. 4:1, emphasis added).

Every form of the word "tempt" in these three verses comes from the root *peirazó,* which is derived from the same root word as *peirasmós.* They all say the same thing: Satan is the source of all *peirazó,* not God. Like the logical argument, the biblical argument from Scripture demonstrates that the "hour of testing" in Revelation 3:10 cannot refer to the wrath of God but, by definition, must be the wrath of Satan.

Christ's revelation to John concerning the last days tells us exactly when the wrath of Satan will test the saints of God, thereby identifying for us the specific period of time referred to as "the hour of testing." Although we looked at this passage before, we need to look at again so that we don't forget it!

> (12) ". . . Woe to the earth and the sea; because *the devil has come down to you, having great wrath,* knowing that he has only a short time." . . . (13:4) and they [the whole earth] worshiped the dragon, because he gave his authority to the beast [Antichrist]; and they worshiped the beast. . . . (5) . . . and authority to act for forty-two months was given to him [Antichrist]. . . . (7) And it was given to

him [Antichrist] to *make war with the saints and to overcome them* ... (Rev. 12:12; 13:4, 5, 7, emphasis added).

The wrath of Satan occurs when Satan gives his authority and power to Antichrist—at the midpoint of the tribulation period—at which time the whole world will be made to choose whom they will serve (the test). Only those who obey the instruction of Christ concerning persecution (the saints "who keep the commandments of God and their faith in Jesus," referred to in Rev. 13:7; cf. 14:12, will be kept from the hour of testing that is to come upon the whole world)—showing us that the context of this passage is the wrath of Satan during the great persecution of Antichrist!

"So, Bob," you might be tempted to say, "you've made your point. The hour of testing, that is, the great tribulation associated with the persecution of Antichrist, is the wrath of Satan not the wrath of God, and it begins at the midpoint of the tribulation period. But doesn't Revelation 3:10 still teach us that Christ will 'keep us from' that hour, not 'protect us during' that hour, regardless of whose wrath it represents?"

Will Keep You From!

Follow with me one more time as we look at this third critical phrase and then you can decide for yourselves. The phrase in its proper context says, "Because you have kept the word of My perseverance, I also will keep you from the hour of testing." In particular, we want to look at the two Greek words that are translated "will keep you from."

"Will keep you from" translates a form of the verb *tēréō,* which is here translated "keep you," and the Greek preposition *ek,* which is here translated "from," because Scripture has already defined what "the hour of testing" refers to.

As we said earlier, the primary meaning of *tēréō* is "to watch over, guard, or keep." In this context, it carries the idea of protecting someone while he is *within* a sphere of danger, not that of keeping him *away from* the danger altogether. Only those who are within a specific sphere of danger need to be watched over or guarded. That is exactly what *tēreō* refers to in this context: guarding those who persevere—who are faithful to Christ—during the hour of testing that will someday come upon the whole earth.

However, it is the shortest Greek word in the entire Revelation 3:10 text, *ek*, translated *from*, that causes all the confusion in the English translation! The confusion is exaggerated by the multiple meanings of the English word "from." Once again, a proper rendering of this little Greek preposition will solve the problem perfectly, bringing absolute harmony to all three phrases that make up our critical text.

I remember a Greek class I was auditing in which we were given a textbook illustration that dealt with Greek prepositions. In the center of the page was a large circle, with straight lines going into, out of, alongside, over, and under the circle. Each line represented a different Greek preposition and illustrated the relationship of that particular preposition to the noun to which it related. The preposition *apó* means "kept outside of, or away from"; therefore, the line on the chart describing *apó* was alongside the circle but never entered it. If something is to be kept *from* something else, *apó* is normally the Greek preposition used. Another line represented the preposition *ek*, and that line began inside the circle and came out of it, representing something that comes "out from the midst of" something else.

In Revelation 3:10, had the writer meant that *those* who followed the teaching of Christ concerning perseverance would be kept outside of the hour of testing, the Greek preposition *apó* would most definitely have been used. The Greek preposition *ek*, however, is the only preposition that pictures deliverance, out from within this sphere of danger, conveying the idea that *those* refers to the faithful men and women who persevere under Antichrist's persecution.

Tēréō ek, used in conjunction, can only refer to guarding or protecting those who persevere while they are *within* the sphere of danger, and then bringing them safely out from the midst of that danger. Thus, the meaning of the text is clear. *Tēréō ek* should be translated, "a watchful protection within the sphere of danger, with a safe deliverance out from the midst of it."

With that meaning in mind, it is interesting to note that this particular Greek preposition *ek*, combined with the Greek noun *peirasmós* (the same Greek word used to describe the hour of testing [*peirasmós*] referred to in Rev. 3:10), are used together in another powerful end time passage we have already looked at several times. It occurs when Peter teaches that

> the Lord knows how to rescue the godly from [*ek*] temptation [test ing—*peirasmós*], and to keep the unrighteous under punishment for the day of judgment (2 Pet. 2:9).

The apostle is not saying that believers will be "kept away from" (*apó*) the hour of testing (*peirasmós*), but that the godly will be rescued "out from the midst of" [*ek*] this time of testing (*peirasmós*). That is exactly the idea in Revelation 3:10, using exactly the same two Greek words!

In a later passage which we looked at carefully in the previous chapter, where the preposition *ek* is once again used in an end time setting, John is told that the great multitude standing before the throne of God

> "are the ones who come out of [*ek*] the great tribulation" (Rev. 7:14b).

As in the 2 Peter passage, this great multitude of believers is not spared the great tribulation by Antichrist, but is delivered "out from the midst of" it, once again picturing exactly what the Greek text intended in Revelation 3:10 (having the same context, the same Greek preposition, exactly the same meaning).

In summary, then, by understanding the Greek of our text, we see that all three critical phrases of Revelation 3:10 demand that the promise that is given to the faithful who follow the instruction of Christ is a promise that is connected with their faithfulness to His teaching on perseverance during Antichrist's persecution, and is a promise that God will guard them while within this sphere of danger and deliver them out from the midst of it. Cause and effect. Because you kept . . . I will also keep. . . .

If ever a single passage argued the case for the prewrath Rapture position, Revelation 3:10 is that passage. Plain and simple! It precisely parallels what is taught by Christ in His Olivet Discourse to His disciples, by Paul in his instruction to the Thessalonian church, by Peter in his instruction to the Gentile aliens scattered throughout the world, and by John in the book of Revelation. It perfectly encompasses the uniform and consistent instruction that God gives to His bond-servants concerning the end times.

Taken or Received?

The next Greek word I want you to look at is found in the Olivet Discourse. When Christ answered His disciples' questions as to when the sign of His coming (*parousía*) and of the end of the age would occur, He answered those questions precisely. Then He gave a very practical history lesson to illustrate His point. Although we have made the comparison several times earlier in this book, we need to look at this critical passage once again and see what the Greek is really saying.

In the middle of the Olivet Discourse, when describing the end of the age, Jesus told His disciples that

(36) "of that day and hour [of Christ's coming, when the sign of the Day of the Lord is given in the sun, moon, and stars]

no one knows, not even the angels of heaven, nor the Son, but the Father alone. (37) *For the coming [parousía] of the Son of Man will be just like the days of Noah.* (38) For as in those days which were before the flood they were eating and drinking, they were marrying and giving in marriage, until the day that Noah entered the ark, (39) and they did not understand until the flood came and took [aírō] them all away; *so shall the coming [parousía] of the Son of Man be.* (40) Then there shall be two men in the field; one will be taken [paralambánō], and one will be left. (41) Two women will be grinding at the mill; one will be taken [paralambánō], and one will be left" (Matt. 24:36–41, emphasis added).

As you may recall from an earlier chapter, Peter also compares the rapture of the godly, and the wrath of God that follows, with Noah and the Flood.

(4) For if God . . . (5) . . . did not spare the ancient world, but preserved Noah, a preacher of righteousness, with seven others, when He brought a flood upon the world of the ungodly . . . (9) then the Lord knows how to rescue the godly from [ek] temptation [testing—*peirasmós*], and to keep the unrighteous under punishment for the day of judgment [the Day of the Lord] (2 Pet. 2:4–5, 9, emphasis added).

Christ makes the same comparison in an earlier conversation with His disciples, saying,

(26) "And just as it happened in the days of Noah, so it shall be also in the days of the Son of Man: (27) they were eating, they were drinking, they were marrying, they were being given in marriage, until the day that Noah entered the ark, and the flood came and destroyed them all. . . . (30) It will be just the same on the day that the Son of Man is revealed" (Luke 17:26–27, 30).

First will be the deliverance of the faithful who persevere under persecution, and then the destruction of those who are left—as in the days of Noah. Two will be together; one will be taken, and one will be left. The truth is plain and straightforward. The ones taken will be the faithful Christians—those who keep Christ's instruction—who will be rescued or raptured "out of the midst of the persecution they are enduring" before the wrath of God begins at the "coming of the Son of Man," just as Noah was removed from a godless, wicked, violent society (Gen. 6:5–12) before the Flood wiped out the world that remained. The ones left at Christ's coming *(parousía)* will be the unbelieving world—left to face the wrath of God, just as in the days of Noah, when God destroyed the wicked by water.

The Pretribulationist's View

But pretribulationists generally take a different view of this passage. Remember, they believe the Olivet Discourse does not apply to the church, but is wholly for Jews and, thus, refers to the battle of Armageddon, not to the rapture of the God's elect. They must therefore make this illustration of Noah and the Flood apply to the battle of Armageddon rather than to the rapture of the saints. For that reason, most pretribulationists claim that "those who are taken" are taken to judgment after the battle of Armageddon. Conversely, "those who are left" will be those who survive God's wrath and enter into the Millennial Kingdom of Christ.

Their argument goes like this: Because the Flood came and *took* the wicked away in judgment (Matt. 24:39), then the one *taken* at the coming *(parousía)* of Christ must in like manner be taken away for judgment (Matt. 24:40) at the battle of Armageddon. That is the only way they can make "the coming [*parousía*] of the Son of Man . . . just like in the days of Noah" tie into their premise that the Olivet Discourse is instruction concerning the coming of Christ at the battle of Armageddon.

The Prewrath View

But is that what the text really teaches? The Greek answers, "No!" The Greek word behind *took* that is used in connection with Noah—"the flood came and *took* them all away"—is from the Greek word *aírō*. But when Christ describes how it will be at "the coming of the Son of Man," when "one will be *taken* and one will be left," the Greek word for *taken* is entirely different. Here the Greek verb is *paralambánō*. That difference is both important and exciting! *Paralambánō* does not mean "to be taken away," as does the Greek verb *aírō*; it means "to embrace or to receive intimately, to or for oneself." It is a compound word, formed from *lambánō* ("to receive from") and *pará* ("beside" or "along side"). Christ uses this word only six times when referring to end time events. Twice in the Olivet Discourse passage (Matt. 24:40–41), three times when the same comparison is made concerning the coming of the Son of Man (Luke 17:34–36), and one time in John 14:3.

Without doubt, John 14:2–3, although not the classic Rapture passage, is certainly the most quoted of all Rapture passages in the New Testament:

> (2) "In My Father's house are many dwelling places; if it were not so, I would have told you; for I go to prepare a place for you. (3) And if I go and prepare a place for you, I will come again, and *receive* you to Myself; that where I am, there you may be also" (John 14:2–3, emphasis added).

"Receive" translates *paralambánō*. Rather than picturing someone who is being taken away to judgment, this Greek verb conveys quite the opposite. *Paralambánō* means to intimately receive someone to oneself, as in the passage above. It would be more than a little confusing, then, if Christ used the word *paralambánō* five times to refer to the wicked being taken away to judgment—which is absolutely contrary to the real intent of the Greek verb—and then the last time used it to refer to the righteous being received in an intimate manner by Himself at the rapture of His saints!

We Who Are Alive and Remain

Another Greek word that cries out to be understood in its proper sense is *perileipómenoi,* for it, too, confirms the teaching of Christ that the elect of God whom He will rescue from Antichrist's persecution can only be the church (see Matt. 24:21–22, 29–31). This Greek word is used only twice in the entire New Testament, both times in the classic Rapture passage given the church in 1 Thessalonians:

> (15) For this we say to you by the word of the Lord, that *we who are alive, and remain* [*perileipómenoi*] until the coming [*parousía*] of the Lord, shall not precede those who have fallen asleep. (16) For the Lord Himself will descend from heaven with a shout, with the voice of the archangel, and with the trumpet of God; and the dead in Christ shall rise first. (17) Then *we who are alive and remain* [*perileipómenoi*] shall be caught up together with them in the clouds to meet the Lord in the air, and thus we shall always be with the Lord. (18) Therefore comfort one another with these words (1 Thess. 4:15–18).

In verses 15 and 17, what the Greek really says is "we, the living, the remaining." At the coming (*parousía*) of Christ, when the church is raptured, the dead in Christ will be raised first, and then we—the living, the surviving—will join the "dead in Christ" in the clouds, to meet the Lord in the air. But why add "the remaining" to the phrase "the living"? For emphasis? It seems redundant—until you check out the meaning of the word in the Greek. As mentioned earlier, the Greek word is *perileipómenoi. Strong's Concordance* says the word means "to leave all around, i.e., *survive.*" In other words, this critical Rapture passage, written for the church, is saying that at the coming of Christ, the dead in Christ will be raised first,

and then we, the living, the surviving, will be caught up together with them—the dead—in the clouds to meet the Lord
in the air!

"Survivors of what?" we may ask. In the context of the Rapture passage given in 1 Thessalonians 4, Paul had been discussing the affliction the church of Thessalonica was undergoing (see 1 Thess. 3:3–5, 7, 13). But in the last days, when the
faithful are raptured out from the midst of the great tribulation,
the living who are raptured at the *parousía* of Christ will be
those who have survived Antichrist's persecution! Thus, a little word used only twice in the entire New Testament, both
times in this classic Rapture passage, gives more clarity to the
text.

Which Way? Over To or Up To?

There is one other Greek word that we need to look at before
we finish this chapter. In its own subtle way, this special word
demands that the Olivet Discourse is speaking of the rapture
of the saints, not of the battle of Armageddon:

> (30) "and then the sign of the Son of Man will appear in the sky,
> and then all the tribes of the earth will mourn, and they will see
> the Son of Man coming on the clouds of the sky with power and
> great glory. (31) And He will send forth His angels with a great
> trumpet and they will *gather together* [*episunágō*] His elect from
> the four winds, from one end of the sky to the other" (Matt. 24:30–
> 31, emphasis added).

Again, the Pretribulationist's View

As stated many times before, those who hold to the pretribulation Rapture position insist that the Olivet Discourse refers
to the battle of Armageddon. They will tell you that the angels
who "gather together" the elect, immediately after the sign is
given in the sun, moon, and stars, are gathering together those

who survive the battle of Armageddon in order to bring them back to the land of Israel.

And Again, the Prewrath View

But, as you have come to know by now, those who hold to the prewrath position see this gathering together as the Rapture of God's elect. The classic Rapture passage recorded in 1 Thessalonians 4:17 says that when the Rapture occurs, we will "be caught up together with them [the dead in Christ] in the clouds to meet the Lord in the air." The peculiar Greek word *episunágō* ("gather together") used by Christ when He speaks to His disciples in the Olivet Discourse will prove that point.

Sunágō comes from two smaller Greek words that together mean "to bring together, come together, gather together, or assemble." It is the root verb from which the noun *sunagōgē* ("synagogue") is derived. Basically, synagogue means a "gathering place," where people assemble together.

In the Olivet Discourse, when we see the Son of Man coming on the clouds and sending His angels to *gather together* His elect, why is the Greek word *episunágō* used to describe this gathering, rather than just the root Greek verb *sunágō*? The answer to this question is very important. Adding the Greek preposition *epí* to the verb *sunágō* gives direction to the gathering. *Epí* basically means "on" or "upon" (just as epidermis refers to the top layer—*epi*—of one's skin—*dermis*). So when this little preposition is added to the verb *sunágō*, it gives an upward direction to the gathering. Therefore, *episunágō* means a gathering together in an upward direction, or "a taking up and bringing together."

You decide. Does that specific Greek word, used only eight times in the entire New Testament, mean a sideways gathering into the land of Israel, or an upward gathering to meet the Lord in the air at the rapture of Christ's saints? It can only mean one thing: exactly what you would take it to mean if the Olivet Discourse is taken at face value. The original Greek text contains an important truth that Christ intended to convey to His disciples, and it is the same truth that Paul clearly conveys to his readers at Thessalonica: that we will be "caught up together . . . to meet the Lord in the air" (1 Thess. 4:17).

And once again, when we compare Scripture with Scripture, we find another clear reference to the Rapture that confirms the use of this special Greek word in the Olivet Discourse of Christ. Remember this passage we looked at in an earlier chapter?

> Now we request you, brethren, with regard to the coming [*parousía*] of our Lord Jesus Christ, and our *gathering together* to Him . . . (2 Thess. 2:1, emphasis added).

In this passage, the "gathering together" to Christ is an undisputed reference to the Rapture of the saints of God. The Greek verb here is *episunágō!* So, once again, the original language argues in favor of the prewrath Rapture position!

Be a Berean!

I realize that this chapter has been somewhat technical. However, I want you to know that working with the Greek and the Hebrew can be an incredibly enjoyable part of studying the Bible. All you need is a good exhaustive concordance, a good translation of the Bible (definitely not a paraphrase), and, if possible, an interlinear Bible that shows the actual Greek and Hebrew words with their English translation printed just below the original text and *Strong's Concordance* reference numbers printed just above.

When you come to a key word in a verse you are working on, check it out in your concordance. Remember, translations are not inspired; the original-language texts were. Each word has only one primary intended meaning in any given context.

Be systematic. Study the way the same author uses a given word in various places in his writings. Then look at how that word is used in similar contexts in other portions of Scripture, by other writers.

Using these readily available language tools will put much information and understanding within your reach. But there is one more resource you must have. God has promised wisdom to those who ask, and the best way to ask for wisdom is on our knees, in humility before Him. We must, as it were, study on our knees!

Dig the meaning of Scripture out for yourself. Compare Scripture with Scripture, words with words, phrases with phrases. This chapter has uncovered only a few nuggets of truth that can confirm or deny positions you are studying. It takes a little common sense and a lot of hard work, but it is more than worth the investment required. And once you get the hang of it—and I assure you, it is not difficult—you will see what a joy it is to carefully study the Bible for yourself.

Check out what your pastor is saying in his sermons. Check out what various reliable authors have written. Check out what is written in this book! Be a Berean. As Luke reports,

> Now these [the Bereans] were more noble-minded than those in Thessalonica, for they received the word with great eagerness, examining the Scriptures daily, to see whether these things [taught by Paul and Silas] were so (Acts 17:11).

So, What's the Big Deal?

I began this book by relating to you the one story I hear time and again, always with the same punch line. "It doesn't matter what I believe; it will all pan out in the end!" Hopefully those of you who have taken the time to work through the previous eight chapters have a different opinion. Perhaps, like myself, you have begun to understand why each critical passage directly tied to Christ's return is accompanied with a severe warning to the reader: "Do not be deceived . . . Do not be misled . . . Read and heed these things . . . Don't take away from the words of this prophecy . . . And don't associate with those who do!"

The study of Christ's coming and the end time events that surround that blessed hope of every genuine Christian is serious business! This is why I have become so passionate when defending things relating to the second coming of Christ. Since the destruction of the temple by Titus in A.D. 70, and the subsequent diaspora of the people of Israel, Christ's return—if Scripture is taken at face value—could not have happened until the Jews once again occupied their own homeland, an event that occurred in

1948, and once again controlled the city of Jerusalem, which occurred nineteen years later in 1967. Now that these two great events are history—exactly as prophesied—the stage has been set for Christ's return for the first time since the end of the first century.

The events that need to happen before a charismatic leader arises out of a northern European nation and makes a treaty with Israel, could occur practically overnight, as it were. Israel still seeks a meaningful peace with her Arab neighbors. Northern Europe still seeks a leader to unite powerful but diverse peoples of different ethnic backgrounds. Men and women have become "lovers of self" (humanism), "lovers of money" (secularism), and "lovers of pleasure" (hedonism) "rather than lovers of God, holding to a form of godliness, although they have denied its power" (2 Tim. 3:2, 4b–5), and the church in general has moved in tandem with the trends of modern society. In many ways, the society in which Noah lived, as described in Genesis 6:5–12, was not unlike the society we live in today!

If ever there was an opportune time for Satan to test the character of the professing church, that time is now! If ever there was a church prone to apostasy, that time is now! If ever the true bond-servants of Christ should be alert and sober, that time is now!

Between now and the coming of Christ, the church must first come face to face with the wrath of Satan through his minion, Antichrist. The true bond-servant of Christ must persevere—follow the instruction of Christ concerning perseverance—so "that the proof of your faith, being more precious than gold which is perishable, even though tested by fire, may be found to result in praise and glory and honor at the revelation of Jesus Christ" (1 Pet. 1:7), "so that when He appears, we may have confidence and not shrink away from Him in shame at His coming" (1 John 2:28)!

The teaching of Christ concerning the persecution the elect will face just prior to His coming is not a popular subject in the "health and wealth" culture that dominates the mind-set of the church today. But, like it or not, a face-value hermeneutic of the passages concerning the return of Christ demands that it will occur, and that when that day arrives, the world will be put to the test to determine whom they will serve, Christ or Antichrist. As we have seen throughout this book, the keystone passage that substantiates this fact is given to us by Christ Himself, in His Olivet Discourse to His disciples. In this discourse Christ presents a careful overview of the events that must occur before He rescues the righteous from the hands of Antichrist and turns His wrath on those who remain when the sign is given in the sun, moon, and stars.

In addition, we have been given Paul's teaching concerning the timing of Christ's return. It parallels precisely the teaching of Christ. Right up front, Paul tells the Thessalonian church that his instruction concerning end time events is "by the word of Lord," and then he proceeds to teach them the same thing Christ taught the disciples in the Olivet Discourse.

And likewise, the book of Revelation—the revelation of Jesus Christ to His bond-servants concerning end time events—like the instruction of Paul, once again parallels the teaching of Christ to His disciples. The same Author giving the same instruction concerning the same end time events.

The Teaching of the Lord through the Twelve Apostles

Because the Olivet Discourse is the focal point in our understanding of the timing of Christ's return, it is interesting to note how the early church looked at this specific teaching of Christ. We find this in an ancient Greek manuscript entitled the *Didaché* or *The Teaching of the Lord through the Twelve Apostles*. Because of the internal evidence of the language used and the subject matter being addressed, Greek scholars have dated the manuscript as having been written sometime between A.D. 70 and A.D. 140. Many scholars prefer the earliest dates (i.e., A.D. 70–90) by virtue of the fact that the author does not quote from

the book of Revelation in the final chapter of the *Didachē,*
something that would have been logical to do had it been in existence when the *Didachē* had been written.

The *Didachē* is a short work, consisting of sixteen chapters
that fall into two parts. The first part gives instruction in Christian living. The second part is a manual of church order. The
early church considered this book, although not inspired, to be
very beneficial reading to every Christian living at that time. It
is interesting to note that the document is filled with allusions
and quotations from both the Old and New Testaments. The
gospel of Matthew is quoted more frequently than any other
part of Scripture, and in particular, the Olivet Discourse.

The entire final chapter of this unusual work (chapter 16,
quoted below) is both a powerful warning and a sober conclusion. It has been translated into English in a work entitled *The
Apostolic Fathers: Revised Greek Texts with Introductions and
English Translations.* I will let this translation speak for itself,
although I have bracketed the specific verses referred to in the
Olivet Discourse (as recorded in Matt. 24). Although not an in-
depth treatise on end time events, it certainly speaks directly
to the intended subject matter and audience to whom the Olivet Discourse was addressed, making the Rapture the focal
point of Christ's instruction, not the battle of Armageddon!

16. Be watchful for your life; let your lamps not be quenched and
your loins not ungirded, but be ye ready; for ye know not the hour
in which our Lord cometh [vv. 36, 44].[1] And ye shall gather your-

1. At this point, John Walvoord (*The Rapture Question,* pp. 53–54), Gerald Stanton
(*Kept from the Hour,* p. 221), and Dwight Pentecost (*Things to Come,* p. 169), three of
the most articulate supporters and defenders of the pretribulation Rapture position, end
their quotation of the *Didachē* in their endeavor to make it look like the *Didachē* sup-
ports the imminent return of Christ. By implication they are attempting to give one the
idea that if the *Didachē* taught imminency, the *Didachē* had to be pretribulational. But
you will quickly see if you read the remainder of chapter 16 of the *Didachē*, the *Didachē*
teaches the absolute opposite of an "any moment" return of Christ. The Lord's coming
cannot occur until after the appearance of the "world-deceiver" *and* the "unholy things"
he will do against "all created mankind," after which those who "endure in their faith
shall be saved [delivered]." Sound familiar?

selves together frequently, seeking what is fitting for your souls; for the whole time of your faith shall not profit you, if ye be not perfected at the last season. For in the last days the false prophets and corrupters shall be multiplied [vv. 5, 11], and the sheep shall be turned into wolves [v. 10], and love shall be turned into hate [v. 11]. For as lawlessness increaseth, they shall hate one another and shall persecute and betray [v. 10]. And then the world-deceiver shall appear as a son of God [v. 15]; and shall work signs and wonders [v. 24], and the earth shall be delivered into his hands [vv. 9, 21]; and he shall do unholy things, which have never been since the world began [vv. 15, 21]. Then all created mankind shall come to the fire of testing [vv. 9, 21], and many shall be offended and perish [vv. 9, 22]; but they that endure in their faith shall be saved [v. 13] by the Curse Himself. And then shall the signs of the truth appear; first a sign of a rift in the heaven [v. 29], then a sign of a voice of a trumpet [v. 31], and thirdly a resurrection of the dead [v. 31]; yet not all, but as it was said: The Lord shall come and all His saints with Him. Then shall the world see the Lord coming upon the clouds of heaven [v. 30].[2]

What further proof does one need? The *Didachē* sees the Olivet Discourse not as a reference to the battle of Armageddon, but as a reference to the second coming of Christ; ". . . ye know not the hour in which our Lord cometh," when "they that endure in their faith shall be saved [delivered]" from "the world-deceiver," from "the fire of testing . . . but they that endure in their faith shall be saved [delivered] . . . then shall the signs of truth appear . . . a sign of a rift in the heaven . . . a voice of a trumpet . . . a resurrection of the dead . . . the Lord coming upon the clouds of heaven."

The early Christians believed this document to be Christ's very teaching passed on to the church through His disciples. Whether this is true is immaterial, but in order for the docu-

2. *The Apostolic Fathers: Revised Greek Texts with Introductions and English Translations*, ed. Michael W. Holmes et al., trans. J. B. Lightfoot and J. R. Harmer (Grand Rapids, Mich.: Baker, 1989), 235.

*ment to be accepted as it was by the earliest followers of Jesus
and His disciples, the teaching in the book must have been consistent with the earliest Christians' memories and understanding of what Christ taught.*

*Clearly the early church believed that the Olivet Discourse of
Christ referred to the rapture of the church. And, just as clearly,
the early church also thought this specific instruction to be important enough to be passed along to all the new converts after
His resurrection. And the Didachē is living proof that it was!*

So, What's the Big Deal?

But if it is really that plain and simple, you may ask, what's the
big deal? Why all the arguments? If the timing of the Rapture is
so clearly revealed in the New Testament, why is there so much
confusion in the church today? Why are people fired from pulpit
ministries, mission agencies, and other parachurch organizations
over this very matter? Why do those who do not hold to the
pretribulation position face expulsion by denominations that
claim to use the same hermeneutic as we do? Do those who begin
to question the pretribulation timing of the Rapture suddenly become heretics because they refuse to blame God for the worst persecution that His elect will ever have to endure since the beginning of time? Do they become heretics, subject to the ridicule of
other professing Christians, because they believe the same thing
that the early church of the first and second centuries believed?

Put that way, in that light, how could any believer treat another
believer with disdain because he or she differs with a view of the
timing of Christ's return that lacks one passage of Scripture to directly support its position? No one would ever admit that it is as
simple as that, but in reality, that is precisely the case.

Background

And why? Let me give you some background that may help
you better understand why this controversy is still such a serious and emotional issue to many.

The pretribulation Rapture position first appeared as a significant theory sometime in the late eighteenth or early nineteenth century, depending on whom you credit it to, and it appeared at a time when all of Scripture was under attack by higher criticism. During the early years of the development of the pretribulation Rapture theory, new cults such as Mormonism, Christian Science, Unitarianism, and Jehovah's Witnesses began to appear, filling the void created by a growing disillusionment with orthodox Christianity. It is not clear who originally worked out the details of this *new view* of Christ's coming, but it has been generally attributed to Edward Irving, father of the Apostolic Catholic Church, circa 1825 (later accused as a heretic because of his low view of Christ), and it was later promoted by John Nelson Darby, one of the founding fathers of the Plymouth Brethren Church in Great Britain, circa 1830, and eventually picked up by Dr. C. I. Scofield during one of his visits to England. It was later taught in his church in Dallas, was popularized by his *Scofield Study Bible* in the early twentieth century, and became the exclusive position of Dallas Theological Seminary and the primary view taught at Moody Bible Institute for the better part of this century.

It should be noted, however, that Dr. Samuel P. Tregelles, the renowned conservative Greek scholar of the nineteenth century (the author of six separate works on translation), considered one of the founding fathers of the Plymouth Brethren Church, strongly disagreed with John Nelson Darby on the position when it first appeared in England. Dr. Tregelles believed in a face-value hermeneutic, and he knew the original languages like few others of his time. In his book *The Hope of Christ's Second Coming* (pp. 74–82), first published in 1864, he denounced the pretribulation Rapture position as being sentimental and emotional and without a thread of biblical support. He stated boldly that the pretribulation "doctrine of the coming of Christ [is] not taught in the Word of God. . . . This whole system stands in distinct contradiction of what the

Scripture reveals" (p. 32). He was doubly concerned about this *new view* because it also promoted a *new position* that made the gospel of Matthew no longer applicable to the church, discarding the gospel into what he called "the Jewish wastepaper basket" (pp. 37–39).[3]

Over the years, Dallas Theological Seminary has produced excellent Bible expositors, all carefully trained in pretribulationism. Since the mid-twentieth century, many graduates of Dallas have become Bible professors and heads of Bible departments in many of our nation's conservative Bible schools, colleges, and seminaries. These men, of course, passed their beliefs on to their students, who then taught their own students, repeating the cycle right up until today. In addition, Dallas has placed many fine pastors in pulpits of churches around the world. If they teach a view on the Rapture to their congregations, it is usually the view they were taught at Dallas. And throughout the years, many of these men have been good friends of my family. In fact, as mentioned earlier, my father was a Christian publisher in the 1940s and 1950s, and he published the writings of some of these fine Bible teachers, including *Systematic Theology* and other works by Dr. Lewis Sperry Chafer, the founding president of Dallas Theological Seminary.

The pretribulation Rapture position is just one facet of the dispensational system that Dallas Seminary has ardently supported throughout the years. But because of the lack of biblical support for their timing of the Rapture, it is perhaps the weakest facet of that system. (Keep in mind that Dr. John Walvoord, past president of Dallas Theological Seminary, has stated in writing that pretribulationism is not explicitly taught in Scripture.) A chain is only as strong as its weakest link, and those who attack a system normally attack what they believe to be the weakest part of that system. Consequently, the best attack against dis-

3. Dr. Samuel P. Tregelles, *The Hope of Christ's Second Coming* (1864).

pensationalism has been, in part, an attack on its timing of Christ's return for His saints.

In order to protect the dispensational system as a whole, Dallas spearheaded a defense that could protect this vulnerable weak link. Consequently, they went along with their nineteenth-century English counterparts and declared that the Olivet Discourse is for Israel, not the church, thus casting that portion of the gospel into Tregelles' "Jewish wastepaper basket." To make sense out of the undisputed sequence of events outlined in the Olivet Discourse, that passage became a reference to the battle of Armageddon, not to the Rapture of the elect; the persecution by Antichrist refers to the wrath of God, not the wrath of Satan; those gathered by the angels of Christ are gathered into the Millennial Kingdom, not up to Christ to meet their Lord in the clouds; those taken are taken to judgment, not received intimately by Christ when He comes to rescue His and destroy the wicked; and so on. They utilized incredible ingenuity in order to defend a position that, in their own words, does not have a single biblical passage to support it. But, in their own words, truth never needs ingenuity to defend it. It stands nicely on its own merits.

Students attending Dallas have been trained to defend pretribulationalism as if their spiritual lives depended on it. In some ways, Dallas professors have even made a person's view of Christ's return a test of one's orthodoxy! And those who break from the ranks of pretribulationism often pay a heavy price and become labeled. In dispensational circles—circles of influence that surround many conservative churches, denominations, colleges, and seminaries in America today—the labeled ones become outcasts. For that reason, many who see the deficiencies of the pretribulation position are reluctant to risk everything to embrace a view that has not received the approval of those who have a degree of control or influence over the institutions they serve.

As I was doing the final editing of this manuscript, I received a letter from a man I have never met, a man who had just read my first book on end time events, *The Sign*. This gentleman's letter so struck at the heart of the issues being discussed in this chapter, I called him and asked permission to quote part of his letter in this book. He agreed. Although he asked that his name be withheld, he admitted that it will be no secret to those who have some knowledge of the man and his church described in his letter. His letter reaches right back into the heyday of pretribulationalism.

> I'm not sure you would know me by name. I've published 14 books in the Christian market, along with one professional book. I was Co-Pastor with Donald Grey Barnhouse [the *only* Co-Pastor Donald Grey Barnhouse ever pastored with] some years ago. . . . Essentially I am writing to thank you for *The Sign* and what it has done for my eschatology! Let me give you some personal background that will sharpen the impact of your work on my life. . . .
>
> I was a card-carrying Scofield Bible Dallas Pre-Trib rapturist. What else in 1940? But three years into the ministry I had severe doubts as to that position. *But in those days one remained silent.* For nearly forty years I would not attempt to teach Revelation inasmuch as I had no established position.
>
> When Donald Barnhouse wanted me to become Co-Pastor with preaching responsibilities, and when he flew me to Philadelphia for a thorough discussion, *I knew he would ask about my eschatology* [he was a strong advocate of the pre-trib position] *and surmised that when I disclosed my doubts* [about the pretribulation timing of the Rapture] *he would retract the invitation.* Indeed it was only hours after my arrival when he asked me questions on eschatology and I laid out my dilemma. At that point Donald became very emphatic, that *he too had questions he couldn't resolve concerning his pre-trib position and reminded me that he had never written a commentary on Revelation.* So he said "Dwight, I hope we both learn more about this as we go along together. But I will continue to preach a pre-trib rapture until then. . . ."

> *Numerous friends who were Dallas men also confessed their doubts.* Then came the book *Pre-Wrath Rapture* and I was on my way to a biblical rational position. Recently my friend here in our area . . . gave me a copy of *The Sign.* I am going through [it] for the third time and find it to answer my questions, providing an entirely credible exposition of *all* the Scriptures. So many, many thanks for your superlative contribution . . . (emphasis added).

No comment from me is necessary. The letter speaks for itself.

There is, however, one other element that contributes to the reluctance of some of these Christian leaders to change their view on the timing of Christ's return for His own, even if they know in the depths of their hearts that their pretribulation position is either wrong or, at best, weak. Teachers and preachers gain significance and stature through what they teach or preach. And if for years they have taught something as truth—and in some cases written books about it—then no matter how overwhelming the argument against their position becomes, it is hard for them to say, "I was wrong." Like Barnhouse, they may admit reservations privately, but not publicly.

Encouragement

The most encouraging comment that I have received to date was from Dr. Walter Kaiser, former dean of faculty at Trinity Seminary. I had been asked to explain the prewrath position to some of the Bible department faculty, as well as to the president and the dean of the seminary. They were very gracious and gave me many hours in two sessions. At that time, I was still in the process of working through this position, and their interaction with me was extremely helpful. Several months later I had the opportunity to spend some time with Dr. Kaiser, one on one. Because he is considered one of the finest Old Testament scholars of our day, I wanted his counsel on the position I was taking, especially as it concerned the Day of the Lord, the signs of which are the focal point of the pre-wrath position.

Unlike almost every book I had read on the second coming of Christ, the central theme of the prewrath position is the Day of the Lord—the sun, moon, and stars being a critical part of understanding when that momentous day—and the events associated with its beginning—commence. I wanted to know if Dr. Kaiser thought that I had taken liberties with these relevant and all-important Old Testament prophecies, as many of the arguments that support the prewrath position were first referred to in the writings of other Old Testament prophets, in particular, Joel, Isaiah, and Ezekiel. His input on the Old Testament foundations upon which I was building the prewrath position, was of great importance to me. The foundations had to be sure and secure, well grounded, and Dr. Kaiser was the engineer who could accurately assess these Old Testament foundations.

His response, which I paraphrase here with his permission, touched my heart warmly. He told me that the prewrath position is the prophetic position that best understands and properly applies Old Testament prophecy concerning the Day of the Lord as it relates to the second coming of Christ. He also stated that he believed that if the fathers of dispensationalism had been able to choose between the pretribulation and the prewrath views, the prewrath position would have received their vote, hands down.

Discouragement

Yet in spite of the strong biblical argument for the prewrath position, and in spite of the consequences of what will happen to the church if the pretribulation view is wrong, scores of men in Christian leadership have told me that if they were to publicly teach the prewrath Rapture position, they would lose their jobs. Marvin Rosenthal (whose relationship with me was discussed in some detail in chapter 2) is a perfect example of what can happen if you change your view. He was thrown out of the Jewish ministry to which he had devoted his life, even though he was personally responsible for building the Friends of Israel ministry from a handful of employees to one of the largest, conservative missions to Jews in the world today. In fact, he was responsible for putting the pretrib position into the doctrinal statement of the mission to begin with! Others have different stories to tell, but each with its own sad ending that is painfully similar to what Marv underwent. These are men who counted the cost, did what they believed to be true to God's Word and, like many others before them over the centuries, paid the price.

Charles Cooper, a Dallas Seminary grad, held a teaching position at Moody Bible Institute. He was extremely popular with the students, was a speaker at Moody Founders Week, at Moody's Pastors Conference, at Bible conferences that sponsored Moody weeks; taught in the day school, the evening school, the Radio School of the Bible; and published articles in *Moody Monthly*. In other words, Charles was highly regarded at MBI. Like Marv Rosenthal, he became convinced of the biblical basis for the prewrath view of Christ's return because of the lack of biblical support for the pretrib position. Because the doctrinal statement of the Institute was premillennial only, not specifically pretribulational, he went public with his position with a clear conscience. But the support base of the school, both academically and financially, was historically pretrib and administration was afraid he would become an embarrassment to the school. Therefore, Charles was given a choice: support the pretrib position and your job is secure; support the prewrath position and you must leave. Moody took no pleasure in forcing the choice and Charles took no pleasure in making the choice. He resigned.

These are only two examples of the stories that I hear from pastors, missionaries, teachers, even board members that have been forced to leave ministries they had given their time and resources to, faithfully, over many years! In every case I know of personally, the individual has sought only to know truth, to try to bring harmony with integrity to the same passages of Scripture we have looked at in the previous chapters of this book. Had the pretribulation Rapture position been a position with a strong biblical basis to begin with, there would have been no need for any of these men to continue to search out the Scriptures for new truth on this issue. But it doesn't so they did. Out of their love for God's Word, they continued their study, knowing in advance that they were risking all for the sake of truth. They were not looking for problems; they were looking for solutions. After diligent study, the prewrath view became their view, knowing in advance that ascribing to a different view other than the pretribulational view, no matter how strong the biblical support, moves you from orthodox to false teacher, just that quickly.

On June 25, 1991 (wouldn't you know it, right on my thirty-first wedding anniversary), an *association of churches* passed Resolution 3, which specifically condemns the prewrath position and one of its staunchest defenders. The brackets are my comments. It reads, in part, as follows:

WHEREAS, Marvin Rosenthal, who formerly served as the executive director of Friends of Israel Gospel Ministry, has published a book, *The Pre-Wrath Rapture of the Church,* which rejects the pretribulation rapture of the Church [that's true]; and

WHEREAS, His thesis declares instead that the Church will be removed just before the fourth quarter of the seventieth week of Daniel [untrue, rather, just the opposite, "of that day and hour, no one knows . . ."], or *just before the Day of the Lord* [true, that's why the position is called "prewrath"]—which he erroneously believes spans the *second half of the last three and a half years of the Tribulation period*—[again, like before, that statement is not accurate]; and

WHEREAS, This false teaching [here he gets labeled a false teacher] ignores the doctrine of the imminency of Jesus' return [that's true] (Titus 2:13; 1 John 3:2–3; 1 Corinthians 1:7; 1 Thessalonians 5:6) [check out these references for yourselves, not one of them deals with the "any moment" return of Christ]; and

WHEREAS, Rosenthal is disseminating this view with hot zeal [that's true of everything he does] and through a periodical titled *Zion's Fire;*

BE IT THEREFORE RESOLVED. . . ."

This resolution reminds me of the accusations brought against Martin Luther because of his simple desire to be biblical. *Sola Scriptura, sola fide!* I'm surprised they didn't include *The Teaching of the Lord through the Twelve Apostles—* the *Didaché* we looked at earlier—on their "hit list" or, for that matter, many of the early church fathers who held to the same position argued in this book. Even Charles Haddon Spurgeon, probably the most quoted nineteenth-century preacher in America today—if not the world—would have made their "hit list" had he been alive when Resolution 3 was put into effect. In a recent article published by Dennis M. Swanson entitled "The Millennial Position of Spurgeon,"[4] he concludes that

Despite claims to the contrary, his [Spurgeon's] position was most closely identifiable with that of historic premillennialism in teaching *the church would experience the tribulation,* the millennial kingdom would be the culmination of God's program (emphasis added).

Later in the text, Swanson goes on to state that the

Key features of historic premillennialism are twofold: (1) the kingdom will be the culmination of the church age and (2) *the "rapture" will follow the tribulation, with the church going*

4. *The Master's Seminary Journal,* Fall 1996, Volume 7, Number 2, pp. 183, 210; Published by The Master's Seminary, Sun Valley, CA 91352.

through the tribulation under the protection of God . . . Spurgeon
fits most consistently in the 'historic or covenantal premillennial'
system (emphasis added).

In other words, Spurgeon too, by definition, "ignore[d] the
doctrine of the imminency of Jesus' return (Resolution 3), seeing the church facing the persecution of Antichrist before the
return of Christ. In doing this, he also "rejects the pretribulation rapture of the church" (again, Resolution 3), thereby becoming, like Marvin Rosenthal, guilty of "false teaching" (and
again, Resolution 3), if indeed Resolution 3 is the inspired
Word of God—which it isn't!

Today, many pastors in this association of churches call us
regularly. They kiddingly refer to themselves as "closet pre-
wrathers," knowing that if they went public with their convic-
tions on this particular issue, they would pay the price and be
expelled from the association, labeled, like Marv Rosenthal,
as proponents of "false teachings." Instead, they encourage
those concerned about end time events to read *The Sign* or *The
Pre-Wrath Rapture of the Church,* letting their people decide
for themselves.

To show you just how serious and widespread this type of in-
timidation can go—and the fear that strikes at the very heart
of those who come under this influence—let me share with you
part of a letter I received from a well-known Bible teacher, not
a part of this particular association of churches but certainly
with a following that would include many within their congregations. This pastor/teacher often quotes Spurgeon in his sermons, championing both the man and his teaching. Again, the
brackets are my comments, intended in part to obscure the
identity of the writer:

God has given to me a group of precious and wonderful people
who serve alongside me. . . . Built into the fabric of all [who serve
in these various ministries] is a commitment to our doctrinal

statement which has been historically pretrib. I don't own these ministries. They belong to the Lord and are a stewardship in the hands of God's people. They are at best fragile—even the church which is so strong spiritually and financially. People all over the world [including many who come under the jurisdiction of Resolution 3] are linked to us. . . . Our commitment to a common belief is our foundation. *If I were to announce that I had become post-trib or pre-wrath, the fragile line that holds* [my ministries] *together could break. Some of the* [leadership of these ministries] *would turn against me. Many* [others] *across this country that feel the kindred spirit and trust us . . . would turn away . . . would go elsewhere. Even our* [peripheral ministries] *would be affected.*

A lot is at stake for me . . . (emphasis added).

In light of Resolution 3, I understand but I don't agree. If you go against the flow, no matter what the truth may be, you will pay the price. Spurgeon was known as a man who stood firm on what he believed the Scriptures taught, no matter how high the cost to himself individually. The final five years of his life were the most difficult, choosing to leave his own denominational union rather than cave in to the Down-Grade controversy.

Oh, my friend, that you were the Spurgeon you preach, concerned more about truth than what "is at stake for me"! What about the sheep you are told to shepherd, about genuine Christians from other churches who come under your teaching, who "feel the kindred spirit and trust" your biblical integrity on an issue as important as this one is? What happens to these "wonderful people who serve alongside you" when they get broadsided with "a great tribulation, such as has not occurred since the beginning of the world until now, nor ever shall" (Matt. 24:21–22a); when those you have promised to shepherd and protect are delivered up "to tribulation and will [be killed] and [will be hated] by all nations on account of My name" (Matt. 24:9); when "many [of those who "trusted" you] will fall away

and will deliver up one another and hate one another . . . and
. . . most people's love [for Christ] grows cold" (Matt. 24:12)?

"But," you say, "a lot is at stake for me." I know; but not for
the reasons you may think.

As the preceding attests, the reaction of those who oppose
the prewrath view has been strong and heated. On an issue as
important as this one, with the consequences that will occur if
one's pretribulational view of the timing of Christ's return is
wrong, it is too bad that it has to be this way. As already noted,
in many ways the prewrath position parallels the pretribulation view. Advocates of both positions are premillennial. Both
positions agree that the church will not undergo the wrath of
God. Both positions believe in a very real Antichrist who will
someday attempt to destroy all who will not submit to either his
lordship or his leadership. In fact, both positions agree on almost every facet of Christ's return except on what comprises
the wrath of God.

The pretribulation position maintains that Antichrist's persecution is part of God's wrath. This not only flies in the face
of what Scripture teaches—that this time is a time of Satan's
wrath—but makes absolutely no sense at all to the logical
mind. Why would God want to vent His wrath upon His precious elect, on those saints who will faithfully persevere—"on
account of My [Christ's] name"—during Antichrist's persecution (Rev. 13)? The very reason they will undergo this terrible
time of Satanic persecution is their refusal to compromise their
relationship to Christ, preferring to "keep the commandments
of God and their faith in Jesus" (Rev. 14:12)! Administering
God's wrath upon these faithful saints is like torturing and
then killing your child for being obedient! If you think about
it, it just doesn't add up! Plain and simple!

On the other hand, the prewrath position sees Antichrist's
persecution as the wrath of Satan against the elect of God for
the simple reason that the elect refuse to submit to Satan's
minion, even in the face of persecution and death. Not only

that, Scripture tells us specifically that this time of persecution will be the wrath of Satan (Rev. 12:12)! How much clearer does it need to be?

Acceptance

In spite of the strong opposition against it, however, the prewrath view is now held by many men and women across our nation and around the world. Our office has received thousands of phone calls over the past several years on our toll-free hot line (1-800-627-5134). Initially, about one out of every thirty calls was from a pastor or teacher. For the past several years, though, one out of every three calls is from men who are *now teaching the position. The Sign* has now been published in Spanish and Russian and requests have been made for Mandrian, Romanian, Hebrew, and German translations. Teaching conferences for church leaders have been given in Romania and Israel, and more conferences have been requested in South Africa, Italy, India, Kenya, Mexico, and Russia. Even students at Dallas Theological Seminary have called to tell us that they hold to the position and are eager to have more information.

Why? Because the prewrath position is based squarely on the Bible, using a hermeneutic that these students, pastors, and teachers know, in the deepest recesses of their hearts, to be the only right way to understand what God is saying in His Word. Unlike the pretribulation view which is not based on the explicit teaching of Scripture and whose "proof at times has been logically invalid or at least unconvincing," the prewrath position rests squarely on Scripture when taken at face value, and for this reason, it is a position that is "logically valid and overwhelmingly convincing"! For these reasons, once you understand the position, you see it throughout the Word of God.

Men and women in the pews are challenging their pastors, using the plain and simple teachings of Scripture to argue their case rather than the confusing teachings of men. Students are challenging their instructors on the basis of God's Word. As a result, those who hold to the pretribulation position have set up committees composed of authors and teachers who have dogmatically supported the pretribulation position for many years. The purpose of these committees is to "tourniquet the patient" before it (the pretrib system) dies from loss of blood. They may succeed in giving the system a temporary transfusion, but without solid biblical support, the patient is on life support and has no hope of genuine recovery.

The prewrath position is not a twentieth-century position. It was the position of Christ. It was the position of Paul. It was the position of Peter. It was the position of John. Even our Lord's revelation to Daniel refers directly to it (see Dan. 12:1–2—in particular the sequence of events and the choice of words used). It was also the position of the early church fathers, including the *Didachē, The Teaching of the Lord through the Twelve Apostles,* which is perhaps the oldest commentary on the Olivet Discourse (i.e., the timing of the Rapture) in existence today.

End time events will occur exactly as revealed in Scripture. Therefore, "See to it that no one misleads you!" "Let no one, in any way deceive you!"

> "Many will come in My [Christ's] name, saying . . . 'The time is at hand'; do not go after them" (Luke 21:8).

Just before the complete and terrible destruction of Sodom and Gomorrah, the Lord said to the angels who were visiting Abraham:

> (17) "Shall I hide from Abraham what I am about to do, (18) since Abraham will surely become a great and mighty nation, and in him all the nations of the earth will be blessed? (19) *For I have chosen him, in order that he may command his children and his*

household after him to keep the way of the LORD by doing righteousness and justice; in order that the LORD may bring upon Abraham what He has spoken about him" (Gen. 18:17–19, emphasis added).

This warning of impending disaster, as well as the reason for it, was given to Abraham not only for his own sake, but also for the sake of "his children and his household after him to keep the way of the Lord by doing righteousness and justice."

My prayer is the same for you, "so that when He appears, we may have confidence and not shrink away from Him in shame at His coming" (1 John 2:28), but rather "the proof of your faith, being more precious than gold which is perishable, even though tested by fire, may be found to result in praise and glory and honor at the revelation of Jesus Christ!" (1 Pet. 1:7).

I rest my case. That's it, plain and simple. "You, brethren, are not in darkness, that the day should overtake you like a thief" (1 Thess. 5:4). You must now decide for yourself.

Original Language Index

agrupneō, 60
aírō, 181
amad (Hebrew), 125
anamenō, 60
ánesis, 118
apekdechomai, 60
apó, 176–177

Didachḗ, 189–192

eggizō, 60
ek, 176–177
ekdechomai, 60
elthon, 160
ekklēsía, 124
eklektós, 80
eltheín, 153–154
epí, 184
episunágō, 184
érchomai, 95, 153
erchómenoi, 159

grēgoreō, 60

hágios, 81
hupo, 148

kataregō, 126

kolobóō, 81
lambánō, 181

pará, 181
paralambánō, 181
parousía, 94–95
peirasmós, 146, 173–174
peirazó, 173–174
perileipómenoi, 182
prosdechomai, 60
prosdokaō, 60

rhúomai, 74

seraphim (Hebrew), 140
skandalízō, 72
sōthḗsetai, 74
sunágō, 184
sunagōgḗ, 184

tēréō, 169
tēréō ek, 175–177
thánatos, 148
thēríon, 149
thlípsis, 71

yôm (Hebrew), 52

Quotes and Referrals Index

Chart Index

In order to answer your questions concerning the contents of this book or to receive additional information, please write:

The Sign Ministries
P.O. Box 113
West Olive, MI 49460

or call toll free:
1-800-627-5134

Robert D. Van Kampen was the founder of Van Kampen Merrit, an investment banking company that sold to Xerox in the mid-1980s. Today, he is financially involved in and on the boards of three separate investment banking organizations, several other unrelated businesses, and also serves as chairman of six Christian mission and ministry organizations. Van Kampen is co-founder of two mission agencies (one concerned with the peoples of Jewish lineage, the other with the untouched, remote area peoples of third world countries), two growing churches, as well as the founder of The Scriptorium, an organization whose sole purpose is the scholastic defense of the authenticity, accuracy, and authority of God's Word, the Bible. In addition, The Van Kampen Collection is the largest private collection of manuscripts, artifacts, scrolls and early printed editions of the Bible in the world today. He holds an honorary doctoral degree in humane letters from Indiana Wesleyan University. He has written *The Sign* (1992) and *The Fourth Reich* (1997).